PRAISE
IMPERFECTLY PERF

C000000146

In a world brimming with chance meetings and fleeting moments, there are those extraordinary encounters that can only be described as serendipitously divine. The day I heard about the "Imperfectly Perfect" and Glenn's efforts was one such moment—a celestial alignment of circumstances that brought together kindred spirits on a path toward something greater than ourselves.

As I opened this book and delved into the stories of the remarkable co-authors, my heart resonated with a symphony of emotions. Tears of recognition flowed freely, for I saw my own narrative intricately interwoven with theirs—each word, each sentiment, each courageous act serving as a testament to our shared humanity. This book, is more than words on paper, these stories are a resounding anthem of self-acceptance, resilience, and empowerment that will leave you not wanting to put the book down.

These stories are not just about words on paper; they are a devine connection between people, so beautifully written armed with vulnerability and boundless determination, to inspire anybody who resonates with amazing authors stories.

This book shows us that our stories, emotions, and dreams intermingle, reminding us that in our imperfections lies our true beauty, and through unity, we can rewrite the narratives that once defined us to help us heal and move forward in life.

EDEN SASSION

BEAUTY & WELLNESS ENTREPRENEUR | ACTRESS

The Imperfectly Perfect Campaign Book Series is a captivating, compelling collection of short stories, one that reminds us that we are each lighthouses who have the power to shine brightly and brilliantly, even on the darkest of nights.

Through tales of grit and grace, this book beautifully captures how individuals have turned trials, tribulations, and travesties into triumphs and transformations, and it will inspire you to do the same!

These stories, brimming with insight and inspiration, shine a radiant beacon of light on the journey of self-discovery. With every story, you'll be reminded of the incredible power that exists not only within others, but also within yourself.

Prepare to be uplifted, inspired, and enlightened! As you read about others who have turned their stumbling blocks into stepping stones, you will be encouraged to fully embrace your story, your life, and yourself. Your life—and your story—like those shared in the this series, has the ability to change both your life and the lives of those around you, too.

The Imperfectly Perfect Campaign Book Series has left an indelible mark on my heart, and I know it will leave an inedible one on yours, too. Run—don't walk—to pick up your copy today!"

ROBERT MACK

IVY-LEAGUE EDUCATED POSITIVE PSYCHOLOGY EXPERT | CELEBRITY HAPPINESS COACH | INTERNATIONAL BEST SELLING AUTHOR ENDORSED BY OPRAH WINFREY, LISA NICHOLLS & VANESSA WILLIAMS

Glenn Marsden has been a beacon of light for mental health awareness. His tireless work with, Imperfectly Perfect has provided a deep look into the lives of celebrities and those of us who suffer on a daily basis with depression, anxiety, ocd, addiction and more. I've personally never felt more seen and understood than I have after reading this incredible book. The message is that we are absolutely enough exactly where we are and more importantly, we're not alone. I am forever grateful to Glenn and Imperfectly Perfect.

GENA LEE NOLIN

AUTHOR, ACTRESS, HEALTH ADVOCATE, FOUNDER "THYROID SEXY".

In a world dominated by overwhelming stress, sleep deprivation, social pressures, and relentless social comparisons, many people struggle, often finding themselves succumbing to feelings of less than.

This distressing trend leads to a surge in depression, anxiety, anger, and tragically, even suicide.

The imperfectly perfect campaign has emerged as a catalyst for change, uniting a community of people who have braved the shadows of their struggles, only to emerge as guiding lights for those ensnared in similar battles to share their stories.

This book stands as a beacon of hope. It offers solace and understanding to anyone grappling with silent suffering, their shame preventing them from seeking help.

This transformative work serves as the inaugural stride towards rediscovering one's true self and the envisioned potential.

Crucially, the book extends its resonance to all individuals. Acknowledging that the pressures of modern life are not exclusive to any one person.

Believe me, this book could be the first step in regaining the real you by understanding you are not alone, you never will be and all you need to do is speak up and seek help and guidance.

Don't be a student of merely reading from this book, master it by applying the steps you take from the stories you read.

KRIS GETHIN
WORLD RENOWNED TRANSFORMATION SPECIALIST, BODYBUILDER, IRONMAN FINISHER, ULTRA-MARATHONER, CEO OF KAGED MUSCLE SUPPLEMENTS, CO-FOUNDER OF THE KRIS GETHIN GYM FRANCHISE & CELEBRITY PERSONAL TRAINER

In a world where challenges seem insurmountable and the odds are stacked against us, there shines a beacon of hope that illuminates the resilience of the human spirit. In the heartfelt pages of this book series, that light burns brighter than ever before.

As I delved into the stories of people who dared to defy destiny, I am reminded of the love and support that both myself and the love of my life, Peter Mills, hold for this extraordinary campaign and Glenn.

Together, we bore witness to Glenn's determination as he carved new avenues for change, even when the odds were stacked against him. Now, as these co-authors come together to share their stories, it serves as a testament to not only their's but Glenn's unyielding spirit to never give up.

With every page turned, tears of inspiration and remembrance fell down my cheeks.

The poignant truth that Peter never had the chance to hold this book in his own hands weighs heavy on my heart.

A heart that still aches from his untimely passing.

I vividly recall the day, just before he slipped away from me, when he shouted over the phone to Glenn his commitment to securing the first copy, and how proud he was of him.

Glenn, my friend, while Peter's physical grasp will never embrace this book, take solace in knowing that his spirit forever embraces what you have done and are doing for many others. His pride in you will always be with you cheering you on and pushing you beyond your limits from where he is.

To those of you who are picking up this book for the first time, I urge you to turn these pages and immerse yourself in the stories and allow yourself to feel deeply. This book is more than a collection of stories; it's a tribute to the human capacity to endure, to triumph, and to persist in the face of adversity and to love"

DIANE MILLS

MENTAL HEALTH ADVOCATE, SPEAKER

IMPERFECTLY PERFECT CAMPAIGN

VOLUME ONE

KMD
BOOKS

A catalogue record for this
work is available from the
National Library of Australia

National Library of Australia Catalogue-in-Publication data:
Imperfectly Perfect Campaign Vol. 1/Glenn Marsden

ISBN:

(Paperback)

CONTENTS

In the pages of this book, you will encounter a collection of deeply personal narratives, each a testament to the raw and honest journeys of individuals. These stories are an unfiltered exploration of adversity, and they delve into the complexities of mental health struggles. Please be mindful that these narratives, while inspiring, may touch on challenging and triggering experiences. Proceed with an open heart and a compassionate spirit as we navigate the profound terrain of these courageous journeys.

BILLY DIB
FOREWORD

I remember as a young boy every night, my father sat my siblings, and I down after prayers, and to share a discussion with us about our faith and religion.

My father would often tell us stories that would prove to us that through faith and submission to God, anything was possible.

During the course of my professional career, I achieved many highs and suffered many lows, but it was my unwavering faith that allowed me to continue to persevere to achieve the great results that helped during the course of my professional career.

In 2015, my faith would once again be tested when my beloved wife Sara was diagnosed with leukaemia and would pass away. It was my faith in God, and knowing that Sara was in a much better place that allowed me to heal and recover from this devastating loss.

Late last year in October 2022. My faith would once again be tested. This time I was diagnosed with non-Hodgkin's Burkitt lymphoma cancer. It was simply through faith, family, friendship, and love that I would overcome this horrible cancer and remain here in this world with my beloved family, my beautiful wife and son.

Faith has been the one thing that has helped me during the course of my life. Simply put, without faith, I don't think that I could have overcome the setbacks I have faced during my life.

Without faith, we have nothing. Faith gives us hope that the future will be bright.

BILLY DIB
2 x World Boxing Champion. WBO Lightweight Oriental Champion & IBF Lightweight
Connect: billydib.com / @ billydib

GLENN MARSDEN
PROLOGUE

I n the quiet solitude of my office, surrounded by shelves lined with books, I find myself reflecting on the incredible journey that has brought me to this moment. The weight of gratitude sits heavy upon my heart, compelling me to pen these words of thanks to all those who have believed in me and the mission placed upon my soul – the Imperfectly Perfect Campaign.

To the public figures, both famous and unsung heroes, who lent their voices to open up the conversations that society so desperately needed, I am eternally grateful. Your courage and commitment to speaking truth have been a guiding light, igniting change in the hearts and minds of many. Without your unwavering support, the Imperfectly Perfect Campaign would have remained a mere whisper in the winds of possibility.

To my beloved wife, my rock and my true support, I owe a debt of gratitude that can never be fully repaid. Your unwavering belief in my vision, your unwavering love and the strength you possess have carried me through the darkest of storms. Your steadfast faith in me has given me the courage to dream beyond the limitations of my own doubt. Thank you for being the foundation upon which our dreams have been built.

To my children, Lincoln and Leighton, you are my constant inspiration, my reason to strive for greatness. In your eyes, I see a reflection of the world I wish to create – a world where compassion, understanding and acceptance reign supreme. It is for you that I fight tirelessly, seeking to leave behind a legacy of change, a world transformed by love and empathy. You are the embodiment of hope, and I am honoured to be your guide on this journey.

A special mention must be made for those who have left this earthly plane, those whose souls graced our lives and brought the Imperfectly Perfect Campaign to life. Your passion, dedication and unwavering commitment to the cause shall never be forgotten. Though your physical presence may be absent, your spirits continue to guide us, urging us forward, reminding us of the urgency and importance of the work that lies ahead. We carry your memory in our hearts as we strive to make your dreams a reality.

Lastly, but certainly not least, I offer my deepest thanks to God, the divine force that orchestrates the symphony of our lives. It is through divine intervention that my heart was opened to see people for people, to recognise the beauty in imperfection and to embrace the complexities that make us human. Through every struggle, every triumph and every moment of doubt, I have felt the hand of God guiding me, instilling in me the unwavering belief that change is possible, that love conquers all.

To all those who have believed in me, thank you. Thank you for seeing the potential within me, for recognising the power of our collective voices and for standing alongside me as we work to create a world that embraces imperfection as the very essence of our humanity.

This is not just my journey; it is ours – a shared mission to heal, to uplift and to rewrite the narrative of our society. Together, let us weave a tapestry of change, imperfectly perfect in its beauty, embracing the uniqueness of every thread. With gratitude in my heart, I take a deep breath and step forward into the unknown, knowing that the road ahead may be challenging but filled with infinite possibility.

Volume one of the Imperfectly Perfect Campaign book series awaits, and it is here that our collective story truly begins …

GLENN MARSDEN
THE MIRROR'S HOLD

As I entered my thirties, a new chapter of my life unfolded before me. I had settled down, embarked on a fulfilling career in the fitness industry and welcomed the joy of fatherhood with the birth of my son, Lincoln. Life seemed to be aligning perfectly, and I relished in the happiness that surrounded me. Little did I know that a storm was brewing within me, threatening to disrupt the tranquility I had come to cherish.

Out of the blue, I found myself fixating on my appearance, consumed by thoughts of body image. This was entirely foreign to me. I had moved to Australia in my early twenties, full of confidence and embracing life to the fullest. I was the first on the beach, revelling in the freedom of shedding clothes without an ounce of self-doubt. The notion of body dysmorphia had never crossed my mind until now.

I stood in front of the mirror, scrutinising every inch of my upper body, comparing myself to others. Why were my arms not as defined as theirs? Why did my chest not resemble the impressive development of those I admired at the gym? These questions echoed relentlessly in my mind, creating a constant chorus of self-doubt. Months turned into a battle against my own reflection, as I found myself sneaking off to bathrooms, seeking solace in the hope of finding a change that would satisfy my relentless self-criticism.

What began as brief moments of self-evaluation escalated into a never-ending cycle of checking and rechecking my appearance. Minutes turned into hours, lost in a perpetual loop of doubt and self-deprecation. I felt as though I was losing control, the grip on my own perception slipping away. The reflection that once held no power over me had become a relentless dictator of my thoughts and emotions.

I kept my struggles hidden, a secret burden that weighed heavily on my shoulders. My wife, the love of my life and the mother of our child, started to notice the change in me. From an external perspective, it must have seemed like narcissism, a self-absorption that contradicted the outgoing, vibrant person I presented to the world.

But it couldn't have been further from the truth. I longed to confide in my friends at the gym, dropping hints about my inner turmoil without fully exposing the depths of my struggles. In hindsight, I can't help but think how frustrating it must have been for them, listening to my repeated complaints of nothing working as effectively for me as it did for them.

My battles with body dysmorphia intensified when my family made the decision to move to Thailand. The unfamiliarity of the new environment, coupled with the additional time I had on my hands, created a breeding ground for the darkness within me to flourish. Removed from the distractions that Sydney had provided, I found myself alone with my thoughts and the mirror, descending into a deeper abyss of self-loathing.

Despite my deteriorating mental state, I continued to convince myself that I was fine. Even when my physique was in peak condition, a testament to my dedication and discipline in the fitness realm, I failed to believe anyone who praised my appearance. My mind played cruel tricks on me, distorting my perception and creating an alternate reality where flaws lurked in every crevice of my being.

Desperate for validation, I relentlessly sought my wife's agreement, pushing her to see the perceived flaws I had convinced myself existed.

When she finally yielded, it sent me spiralling into a new level of certainty. The words, 'I agree,' became a distorted lifeline, a confirmation that my insecurities were justified. I clung to those words as proof that I wasn't crazy, that I wasn't alone in my assessment of myself.

But one day, everything changed. My wife, with a mix of concern and determination, sat me down and delivered a heartfelt ultimatum. She expressed her love for me, but also her growing frustration and concern for our relationship and our child. She told me that if I didn't seek help, we would have to part ways because I was losing myself to the mirror, neglecting the role of husband and father that she cherished in me.

In that moment, I broke down. Tears streamed down my face, and I wept with a mixture of relief and despair. The realisation of the toll my obsession had taken on my loved ones hit me with an overwhelming force. It was a wake-up call, the jolt I needed to recognise the severity of my condition and the urgency to seek help.

That day marked the beginning of my survival. It was the catalyst that propelled me towards a path of healing and self-discovery. I sought therapy, allowing a trained professional to guide me through the maze of distorted thoughts and emotions.

I learned to separate my worth from my appearance, to embrace self-acceptance and self-compassion. It was a challenging journey, but one that proved transformative. It was also a time when I realised that my worth had been tied to comparing myself to others on social media. I made the decision to turn it off, to disconnect from the toxic world of comparison and unattainable standards.

But turning off social media wasn't enough. I needed to face my own demons head-on. During one of my therapy sessions, the psychologist tried to attach my distorted thoughts to my childhood, as if the struggles I faced were solely a result of my upbringing. It infuriated me. I knew deep down that this battle with body dysmorphia was intricately woven into the complexities of societal expectations and the toxic masculinity we are raised to believe in.

And then, almost five years ago, I received news that shattered me to my core. An old friend from the UK had passed away. His social media accounts portrayed a life adored – family, holidays, cars and a successful career. But as I scrolled through his posts, I stumbled upon a video that stopped me in my tracks. It was a heartwarming moment of him and his little boy laughing and cuddling, a glimpse into a love-filled father-son bond.

That video broke my heart because I knew that little boy would never see his dad again. The realisation hit me like a ton of bricks. The weight of the emotional burden that my struggles had imposed on my own family suddenly felt insurmountable. The thought of having to tell a child that their father was gone, to witness their world shatter in an instant, was unfathomable.

It was in that moment that everything clicked into place. The journey I had been on, combined with this heartbreaking revelation, led to the birth of the Imperfectly Perfect campaign. It became a movement aimed at dismantling societal expectations, challenging the toxic narratives that perpetuate body image issues and mental health struggles.

Imperfectly Perfect became a platform for people to share their stories. It became a space where vulnerability was embraced and compassion reigned supreme. It was through this campaign that I found solace in knowing that I wasn't alone in my struggles and that by opening up, we could offer support to those who were silently suffering.

My own journey became intertwined with the larger tapestry of the human experience. I realised that our flaws and imperfections didn't define us but rather served as reminders of our strength and resilience. Imperfectly Perfect wasn't about striving for perfection – it was about accepting ourselves as flawed, beautiful beings and supporting one another on our shared path of healing and self-discovery.

Returning to social media with a new perspective, the Imperfectly

Perfect campaign became a voice for change.

It encouraged others to challenge societal norms, to break free from the shackles of comparison and to embrace their own unique journey. The response was overwhelming. Messages of gratitude and solidarity flooded in, a testament to the power of vulnerability and the impact of genuine connection.

Today, I stand as a survivor, armed with the knowledge that my value extends far beyond my physical appearance. I have reclaimed my life from the relentless grip of body dysmorphia, and as I reflect on those dark days, I can't help but feel grateful for the love and support that surrounded me. My wife, in her unwavering commitment, never gave up on me. She saw beyond the shadows that consumed me and believed in the person I could become. Together, we rebuilt the foundation of our relationship, fostering understanding, empathy and open communication.

What I will point out here, as I navigated my healing journey, was that there were moments when I suddenly felt an inexplicable sense of guidance, as if something greater than myself was gently leading me forward, events happening to me which were in my eyes, unexplainable, serendipitous occurrences surrounding me daily and people contacting me from around the world, claiming that this was all being divinely guided.

I'll be honest, at first I laughed, as like anything in this world, what you don't know, you truly don't know. So all of these words being fed into me was something unbeknownst to myself the very thing that seemed to be confirming all that I was innately feeling.

Looking back, I realise that God had been with me all along, orchestrating events and connections that I had not fully understood or recognised at the time. I wasn't brought up with faith, I wasn't spiritual and I would never claim to be religious in any way, shape or form. But what I did realise along my path was that every step on my journey was being guided and the more I built a personal relationship with God and leant into it, the more I was understanding my purpose.

For me, this chapter of my life forever serves as a reminder of the resilience of the human spirit, the power of connection and the unyielding strength found within the depths of our souls.

Through the mirror's hold, I myself emerged with a new-found purpose, a burning desire to create change and inspire others to break free. I discovered that Imperfectly Perfect stood alone in its mission to create lasting change and build a legacy of support and empathy. It was more than just a passing trend – it was a testament to God's presence in our lives and His call for us to help one another through our stories.

I witnessed the power of vulnerability and the way it connected people on a profound level when stories were shared. The campaign became a reminder that God works in mysterious ways, using our imperfections and our pain to bring about beauty and transformation. It became a space where people from all walks of life could come together, transcending societal barriers and embracing the shared humanity that unites us all. It extended to every individual, regardless of their past or present circumstances. It recognised that our challenges, adversities and addictions are not meant to be judged or chastised, but rather transformed into blessings that can serve as a source of support and inspiration for others who may be going through similar struggles.

Together, we can and will rewrite the narrative and build a world that celebrates our imperfectly perfect selves and through God's guiding hand, Imperfectly Perfect will continue to stand the test of time, building a legacy of resilience, connection and support. It will be a testament to the power of our stories and our shared humanity.

Together, we can make a difference, one story at a time, knowing that our personal journeys and the challenges we have faced can become beacons of hope for those who may be struggling.

Through Imperfectly Perfect and now our book series, we extend God's love and grace to all, shining a light in the darkness and reminding others that they are not alone, they will not be judged and our stories will serve as a source of support and inspiration for others who may be going through similar struggles.

GLENN MARSDEN

Founder of Imperfectly Perfect Campaign | Motivational Speaker

Connect: imperfectlyperfectcampaign.org | from pagetostage.co | @imperfectlyperfectcampaign | @_glennmarsden

RACHAEL NEWSHAM
CREATIVITY IS A GUT FEELING & SO IS LIFE

Happy hour isn't at the pub, it's at the club. The health club. I squat, lunge, dance, punch and kick my heart out, in front of whoever turns up for that time slot.

I never intended for it to be happy hour, but as I look back at the last twenty-plus years, it's what I serve up and exactly where I've spent the majority of my time so I've realised that's what it is. Consistently showing up to teach a training session and inadvertently service not just the bodies, but the hearts and minds of the restless who wander into my studio looking to get their step count up, their sweat on and take off the day's worries. I wonder if you've ever been in my class.

Have you ever met a 5'5.5" (although I may have lost that crucial half by now) woman with a very weird accent that sounds half n' half? A full measure of northern English mixed with a shot of antipodean. Her jokes are lame, but she laughs at them and so does the class in hope that it delays her from the inevitable intensity of the workout she has happily crafted from the world of mixed martial arts inspired fitness. If you've never heard of me and this book fell into your hands, then hi I'm Rach Newsham. A Lancashire lass from the United Kingdom who emigrated to Hobbiton (aka Aotearoa, New Zealand) in 2004 to pursue a once-in-a-lifetime career opportunity teaching group fitness. Born on the borders between gen-X and the millennials, with a cheeky sense of humour and way too shy to make the most of life and get amongst it for the most part of growing up, until she found her feet in the gym. Nice to meet you.

The fitness industry is where I've spent my years, working alongside some epic people. Absolute legends of their game. If you worked in the industry, you'd know them: Emma Barry, Steve Renata, Pete Manual, Mike McSweeney, Yvette Flacke and Dan Cohen to name but a few. I could fill this whole chapter with the names of people who have inspired me over the years. If you want to know how I became me, take a look at who mentored me, and there's page two of the blueprint to my greatness, page one being my family, friends teachers and coaches of every sport and art mum got me involved in whilst she was my boss (haha). I've never called her that and certainly wouldn't dare in person, but here it is, Mum, from a safe distance, that being a whole ocean away, you definitely were my first boss!

Striving for perfection for as long as I can remember in my childhood and as a young adult, it served me well. I worked through the shyness with discipline. Something I can thank both my parents for. Absolute beacons of strength and resilience. World-class humans and hard workers, both of them. A theatre sister for the NHS and a sparky entrepreneur sole trader. Cheers, Mum and Dad. Even though at the time you did my head in (northern English slang for frustration) because there was little wriggle room for slacking off my dance/keyboard/swimming/athletics class and sitting in front of the TV. Nowadays I can recognise you probably didn't want to go to class either, but you stayed the course to make sure I did, and for that you have my total respect. How you did all that after a full day's work for me, is just pure love. You didn't have to. I didn't have to. Somehow you got me there and kept me there. Legends! Thanks to you I had such a head start in life.

After all the physical growing up was pretty much done and dusted, the mental growth kicked in for me, and it's not even remotely close to the growing pains in my legs I used to just shake off and force myself to ignore and fall asleep. These growing pains can't be ignored. No amount of paracetamol crushed up on a spoonful of raspberry jam or pamol syrup was going to ease these aches and pains. The whole mental growth comes in waves of ouchy moments. The type of ouchy when you feel let down, disappointed, distressed, disillusioned, disadvantaged. A bit of a dickhead too, for willingly and naively getting on the worst emotional roller-coaster ride of your life, time after time being schooled the hardest lessons, by life, otherwise known as other folks also on their journey in life. It is what it is, as the saying goes. The saying that got me moving and kept me moving.

As I look back now across the time line of my life, at some of the times I was feeling fed up and lost, over the last twenty years building a life, I wish I had known that I was just living a real and full life, and I wasn't getting 'it' wrong. I was purely growing. Keeping going as I did, time after time, was all part and parcel of sending me towards the proverbial tomorrow. I wish I had been given a book like this to read that pulls back the curtain on the big stage of life and reveals that it's not all spotlight and stardust. I can't help but think that if I had watched less Disney happily ever after movies and read more real-life writings, I would have worried less about whether or not I was 'getting life right', and just picked myself up faster. Inevitably, however, I did, and I'm stoked at what I've accomplished in life to date. Looking ahead, my mission and ambition is steeped in spreading the sauce and spilling the tea on living your best imperfectly perfect life if you are so much as brave enough to do so. I've discovered that me being me is the way to be if I want to do that.

The moment I stumbled across the Imperfectly Perfect campaign I knew I had found my people. I was tired of scrolling through the 'gram life with a lens on it. I craved something real, and I worried that we as a society were sliding down the slopes of dissatisfaction into Fakeville. Social media popularity was polling highly around the mid-2010s in the form of a very sweet shot of lifestyle and glam living that left an aftertaste of ick behind. It didn't feel right to me. The whole advertising yourself by means of a public journal where the entries are multiple photos of you standing weirdly arching your back, sticking your leg out at an awkward angle and duck-face pouting off into the distance with a random quote attached below, besides hashtags for days.

As I write and read back, I'm reminded of where my head was at when the 'gram was just getting going. I knew if I posed this way or that way as such, I'd join the fitspo movement, but it just felt hard. Like swimming uphill. Yea, that hard. Because running uphill is hard enough, but swimming must be harder? I've never seen a pool on an incline though so let's be real and confirm my metaphor is just that. I'd hate anyone to think I actually believe in incline pools. I just know swimming one lap is far harder than running one so point made on how hard the fitspo life felt to me. The 'gram kind of started off as something fun and a way to keep in touch with friends and family and discover who the hottie is from across the road at the other office. Absolute dreamboat, by the way, he was. The most smoking-hot smile that made my head turn, every, darn, time just by walking past him. He had effortless smouldering energy, but unfortunately for me, I wasn't the oxygen he was looking for to light that flame up. I found out who the tall, dark and handsome man was shortly before he left to the see the world and play for an overseas sports team. I digress. Back to the 'gram!

It steadily deteriorated for a while, with every post from who you follow the same as the last. A selfie here, a selfie there, a selfie taken everywhere and nothing captivating beyond a fresh meme or quote that felt like it hadn't been said before. Then it seemed to quickly escalate into the world's largest popularity contest. Everyone grafting to get followers. Changing their posts to appeal to whatever seemed to work the best and get them more engagement. Oooh, now there's a pop cult word of the era too. *Engagement.* This word to me always meant something two people did as a form of commitment to each other. A prelude to a life of the same hand-holding morning cuddles and dodgy birthday gifts for life. I will spare you the other beliefs I have around that for this chapter and another book. Back to the 'gram again and it's new identity as a popularity contest.

I was never a fan of individual event competitions, so this was red flag city for me. Much rather preferred a team event or show, where any win is done as part of a team. I used to squirm under the spotlight because the butterflies were too much for me. Don't let me lead you astray and leave you thinking I didn't partake in the early excitement of social media madness, because I did. I have plenty of random posts from way back that I can happily say some hardcore fans would have to seriously scroll to see, thank goodness lol. However, it didn't last too long, so there's not too many. To coin the gen-Z's catchphrase, it gave me the ick. I didn't think of it like that back then but that's exactly what it was for me. An uncomfortable feeling. The world placed emphasis on sharing every piece of your day if you were someone of interest in some way, and no-one was too perturbed by it. It was the newspaper of its day. A daily report of everyone's dinner plans. A degustation of behind the scenes of daily life, and to me it just felt like too much. Part of me felt I was being left behind by not posting all that faff and the larger part of me felt so much better for not. In fact, I felt like the odd one out for a good while because I wasn't hot to post on the 'gram. I remember sitting down for dinner on tour once, and one of the team we were working with/for asked me if I was going to post where I was tonight and the food that had just been placed in front of me. I politely said no and then went off on one to explain myself away, whilst watching their vacant glare shine right through me into my soul. I could hear my inner voice saying, *Rach, the whole point of you being here was to raise the volume on the product we were all endorsing, and you are blatantly declining to even whisper about it?! No wonder they are enquiring, and very politely, may I add?* It just felt icky to me. The attention thing felt wrong and that's all I knew. I imagined myself walking up to strangers around the streets holding up a filtered and captioned image of myself and saying, 'Hey, look at me and like it and comment please,' and lol that just was ridiculous to imagine. That was what I was essentially doing if I was to post all that faff and nonsense, and it felt embarrassing in the real world, so on that basis I wrote it off as just not feasible in the virtual world of the 'gram.

None the less it was an important up-and-coming form of communication and I was a bit of an early adopter amongst my peers , dare I say it, of Twitter and the 'gram. A friend of mine who I considered to be the epitome of early adoption on the tech front hadn't got onto either. He was responsible for me and many others in Aotearoa migrating away from the Nokia 5510 or whatever it was, onto the iPhone. So anyway, back to the 'gram that I had now lost all momentum with yet needed to go full steam ahead and enter #BadBoySteveSteve.

Stevie Ox was on the scene somehow and I can't remember how we knew of him at the time, but he was suggested as a social media manager for me to help me post more. Naturally being open-minded I agreed and said, 'Yea, sweet, let's do this!' after we'd had a coffee and vibe checked. NB back then it wasn't called a vibe check but in 2023 terms I now know that's what we were doing, and we got on and it seemed like a great solution. It was a great solution. Stevie had energy and a professional camera, and we did one of those photoshoots down at the park and he'd upload a stack of photos for me to choose from. They all looked ace. He was great. So now you are wondering what happened. I basically still couldn't post. He'd have all these hashtags ready and after a few posts it started to feel in conflict with me in terms of how I was on a day-to-day basis. So, whatever was going on for me personally would feel like it was jarring with whatever was on the plan to post that day. For example, if we had stuff to post that was all hype and happy but I'd just had a bunch of stuff dropped on me from a big height, I didn't really feel like posting hype and happy. Stevie suggested I look at it like personal and business and just separate them mentally. I tried. I failed. I am the same person whether I'm at work or at home. It's still me. It's still my feelings. I'm not a cereal box or a treadmill, and he's also not wrong at all to suggest what he did to help me. It just didn't work for me that way. Other folks didn't seem to have a problem in my eyes, because everyone appeared to be able to post one after the other after the other, but I couldn't comfortably do that. I definitely could have done these posts had my life depended on it, but it was super uncomfortable. I don't enjoy that feeling. To me it felt disingenuous. When I broke it down at the time I concluded that a business isn't a human, so it shouldn't have feelings, but still I couldn't 'post-post'. Yea, that's my attempt to write in 'millennialease'. When they go out for a few drinks or dinner with friends and then stay out and play hard, with their best clothes and accessories, they call it 'out-out'. So, for me to post hard on the 'gram is coined a 'post-post'. Let's see if that carries on. Let's see if that's 'lit fam'. Honestly, smh to the new lingo. Speaking of lingo, one of the hashtags that Stevie wanted me to use on a post was #badgirlrachrach and I absolutely cracked up laughing. I'm not sure if we actually did or not, but it was around the time Rihanna was dropping tune after tune and I think she had an album and possibly her own hashtag, #badgirlRiri . I told some of my friends and they howled with laughter. Rihanna is a total badass, but I didn't think of myself as being comparable to her, badass or not! After this, Stevie would be known to me and my circle as badboystevesteve. Surprisingly enough, our time together as a social media duo was short-lived. He got a fantastic opportunity come up and now runs his own dreampark space for creatives. I would have been a painful client for him. I couldn't post what he recommended and at the rate he did either. I also couldn't let him take over my profile and do it for me, because that felt disingenuous and icky. Looking back and reflecting on all my thoughts and feelings, I was really on point and ahead of the curve of thinking, just not able to put a label on it. These days, businesses are expected to behave conscientiously online, demonstrate they have feelings and opinions and take a stand against old ways and outdated thinking and behaviours. For example, if the world is addressing a negative social construct online because of someone experiencing something painful and unjust, then it would be considered poor taste and not reading the metaphorical room to post something hype and happy that flew in the face of the current world climate. You could post something (in my opinion) but it would have to address the fact that you showed awareness of the online climate, so you didn't come across as rude or ignorant.

I'm glad I could feel or sense this expectation back then even if I didn't understand it, and through my own gut instincts, take action, even when I couldn't put a label on it. Others couldn't appreciate it right then and there, but retrospectively they have since then. I guess the takeaway here is to trust your gut instincts or feelings, even if you can't make sense of it so others comprehend your point of view. Not everything is understood at the present time. I've said for a while that I feel my life appears to be lived forwards and understood backwards. Lots of biggish things happen that I can't make sense of until enough time has passed and then I look back and can see what was happening and why. I've packed a lifetime of learnings into the first twenty years of real adulthood and weathered so many growing pains that I couldn't see coming but now totally could, from a country mile away. Would I change it? Certainly not.

Every chapter so far in life isn't measured in chronological years for me, it's measured by moments or memories. Some joyful and some painful. This would be the same, I expect, for anyone else reading this chapter. Many years ago I would have said yes to the option to go back and change the past, but with experience on my side, I can now see that the person sitting here today, typing out a chapter of life for anyone interested in a snippet of my imperfectly perfect life history, can recognise that all those growing pains were helping me become the me I am today, the me I was always going to be. I'm proud of me. I love the me that I have become. I know some of my earliest days I was naive or green in terms of business etiquette and asked questions innocently from a place of enthusiasm or concern that I just wouldn't say in the same way now, like, 'How can you be so sure your opinion is the right one given that you don't teach this workout?' to someone very senior to me. Hahahaha, oh my gosh cringe. However, looking back, had I not said what was across my heart I would have been hiding who I am. I'm a heart full type of person. I take care with you with the assumption you are going to take care with me, until you show me differently. So you can trust that whatever I'm saying, if it makes sense to you or not, the intention is always for the greater good. How can you be so sure? Because I've learned that we reap what we sow, and I don't want any bad karma in my backpack, thank you. I'm not saying I'm a good gardener by any stretch of the imagination, so I do plant with the hope things grow, and then learn by experience whether I made the environment good for growth or not along the way. I also like to hike without a heavy backpack. Are you keeping up with my string of metaphors? If you are, well done, that puts you in the top percentile of society. Most people give up. How do I know this? You'd need to refer to Newsham, R (2002) Why you should not be a dick: A longitudinal study of human behaviour using a single case. *The journal of the life season after season, Rachael Newsham* p22. There's no DOI because I haven't gone digital, so you'd have to request access. Hahaha I could keep this going as it has a certain ring to it but I'm making myself laugh. For transparency, that's how you cite someone else's words/work using the APA referencing format that universities use that has driven me nuts since I went back to university in 2022 to do a part-time course.

The biggest repeat lesson I continue learning in life so far is to put my needs first. Writing for the Imperfectly Perfect campaign book series was typically a very drawn-out decision for me. On face value, it was a brilliant opportunity, but the dominant thought on replay in my head was I had so much to do and didn't want to let anyone down. Rather than, *Wow, how cool!* It was, *Whoa, can you manage all this with so much change management going on at work and that GDAP at The University of Auckland to do on top of work and other stuff. Don't be the person, Rach, that says yes then must renege and let the team down.* Well, cutting to the chase, you can see I learned the lesson about putting myself first and wrote a little chapter. I'm chuffed I did too because I completed something from my list of things I wanted to do. Not the list of things I need to do for work, but the list of things I wanted to do for myself, and the kickback happy vibes that come from just giving something your best shot are super worth it. I didn't know whether or not I could make a chapter interesting enough to be good enough, but in hindsight, just starting and then continuing with an imperfectly perfect attitude enabled me to get it done. For context, it was written from the departure lounge at JFK airport in NYC at a coffee shop, then on the plane, then on the Manchester airport train, then at my mum's kitchen bench, then at the coffee shop in the village. That's my travelling life and how I've spent my non-teaching time for the last twenty years, so it was indicative of my life and also very refreshing to have something more self-focused to concentrate on other than filling my travelling time with music and movement.

In closing I have many life learnings. We tend to learn by example. A great human called Pete Manual once told me I should 'be what you want to see', and that stuck with me. It's been a pillar of value throughout my career thus far. An anchor during storms when I could lose my way and play up rather than pull together. I've learned that taste buds evolve faster than humans evolve. So keep trying new foods and other opportunities, folks, as you may like stuff you didn't before. Keep in mind, humans changing who they are takes a whole lot more time than taste buds. I hated olives until a mate of mine had a bowl on his benchtop one night we were all over for drinks. I was starving, and knew that unless I ate something, the drinkies were going to end my night earlier than I had hoped for. I tried them and couldn't believe how yum they tasted! And now for an example of humans taking longer to change is me taking some people at their word that they've changed, only to learn they were just saying that in full knowledge they were never going to stop doing what they were doing, because it was way too hard for them, but they didn't want to lose me or their power over me. Leading me to believe they were changed was just as good as actually changing and bought them time to continue that behaviour. They volunteered that information to me down the line after being caught out for the umpteenth time so that's how I have confirmation on that. Personally, I can also confirm the struggle to change my own behaviours with my own experiences is very hard to do. I've tried several times to be an emotionally unattached human that can make cold hard calls or decisions, but I fail more times than I succeed. Doing this exercise helped me realise I can't very easily change who I am either. Even with huge benefit to me, it's a struggle to rewire behaviours. Especially those that feel inherently good for both me and society but cost me far too high a metaphorical price to sustain or maintain. Learning this lesson helped me have compassion towards others who have behaviours they'd do well to lose but can't seem too either. From a first-hand experience, it's hard.

So, each to their own on this fabulous ride we call life, in the knowledge and belief that we are all capable of growing and change but in our own sweet or divine timing. When we get sick and tired of being sick and tired, or when the loss is so huge that we can't possibly lose anymore or afford to, we change, we grow. The greatest restriction and time-waster is striving for perfection before stepping forward in life. Living in the imperfectly perfect way allows for error and course correction. Allows for small tentative steps forwards that may be awesome and may also be awful. Recognising that everyone I interact with is also on the path of that imperfectly perfect life. For any of you reading this wondering if there are answers here to help them, I'd encourage you to quit waiting and start creating that life you deserve. The answers aren't in a book, or online or at the end of your perfect life. They are discovered at the edge of life where the risk reward scale is, where the tears of sorrow and joy live. The answers are a product of asking the universe a question, so make a decision to go and do something and see what happens. Once you start asking the universe questions by taking action, the answers will reveal themselves in due course. You won't win them all but neither would you want to. Living a human life is to experience all that being human is, which is a spectrum of triumph and trauma. Living an imperfectly perfect life is a privilege we grant ourselves. Go live yours, folks.

RACHAEL NEWSHAM

Director | Choreographer | Presenter | Speaker | International Health & Fitness Coach | Celebrity Fitness Trainer
Connect: @rachael_newsham

JEREMY JACKSON
JOURNEY OF A SOUL WARRIOR

Imagine a teenage boy on the streets of an impoverished and broken city, far from the beautiful beaches and happy hum of his home. The brokenness of the city speaks to him; it feels like the only home he is worthy of having, as it allows him to disappear into its decrepit streets without bother or question. He sits on the grimy curb in the same clothes he dressed himself in last week with his head in his hands - guilt-ridden, full of shame, 30 pounds underweight, with a pimply face, greasy hair, and Skeletor cheekbones. The critic in his mind screeches at him, like nails on a chalkboard, reminding him that his livelihood and security depend on his appearance, the appearance he has allowed to fall to ruin. All of his worth and potential success are tangled up in his ability to rise to what he was born and bred to do: look good and entertain. He had failed utterly.

This same boy was once living a life beyond the wildest of dreams with more success, fortune, and adoration than most people will ever see in their entire lifetime. He was once surrounded by beautiful people, traveling to the most exotic places in the world, and being fawned over by seas of young women. However, it wasn't enough. It obviously wasn't enough. And it wasn't until he found himself in the deepest depths of despair that he was forced to find a way out. And through that triumph, this boy has become a man, and that man, a Soul Warrior. That boy, turned man, turned Soul Warrior, is me.

We all have a story to tell; each one packed with a plethora of experiences. These experiences may be characterized by the most victorious and delicious joy, the deep, dark crevices of immeasurable pain and suffering, or anything else in between. This one is no different, though its peaks and valleys may stretch farther than most. Anyone can triumphantly access the power of utilizing the various pieces of their story to emerge as their best self. And sharing this message is what it means to be a Soul Warrior; someone who passionately and bravely fights for Light and Truth, unwavering in their purpose.

A Soul Warrior is someone who fights not for personal gain or for material rewards but to demonstrate Divine Purpose, Love, Wisdom, and Truth from within. He fights with all his might, even when it appears the battle cannot truly be won or may never be understood by others. A Soul Warrior is persistent in seeking this Divine connection, careful not to succumb to the worldly clamors that constantly bang at his door. It takes work, unending surrender, and most importantly, the absolute readiness to share this lifestyle with others who wish to overcome their own personal prisons so that they too may become a Soul Warrior.

I will tell you a bit more about how I got here. I grew up in a broken home, never knowing my father and dead set on rebelling against my single mother who loved me beyond words. In an attempt to find an outlet for my rambunctious, inquisitive, hyperactive, eccentric, and theatrical tendencies, my mother dedicated all of her time to caravanning me to various television auditions. Since I was in diapers, I dreamed of standing on stages and entertaining as the audience fell to their knees, much like they did for Elvis Presley and Michael Jackson. I tirelessly practiced my dance moves, accents, songs, and costumes. And when my mother recognized that I would not pay attention to anything else like I did to this craft, she decided it was time to attempt to give me what I had dreamed of.

At a young age, I was determined to achieve great things. From age six to 10, I was in over 60 television commercials, on the cover of various computer game packaging and children's magazines, had landed roles in major motion pictures, and was a highly sought-after child actor. By age 10, I was swept up in the current of stardom, as I landed a role as a main character in the hit television series, Baywatch.

As I mentioned earlier, I have seen life in the most glamorous and fantastic of ways. I was a magnet to beautiful women, fast cars, and good fortune. But I clung to the credo of performance-based values, which I didn't realize would ultimately be my downfall. In our current social climate, almost everyone is working to have "enough." We say things to ourselves like, "I will be happy once I have enough..." of something, anything. This ceaseless search for "enough" propelled me into a seemingly endless state of exhaustion, as "enough" never came. It has been revealed to me that working hard enough, and being good enough, will only reward me with fleeting feelings of achievement that will have to be won over and over again to sustain themselves. The price of this delusion has never been worth the temporary material gains I have seen, as it eventually consumed me - mind, body, and soul.

I worked hard, I was good at my craft, and it felt rewarding for a time. While I had no ability to conceptualize it back then, no amount of money and material goods could fill the void or soothe the ache deep within my soul. The great wealth of accolades and achievements that surrounded me would never make me feel whole. Eventually, I searched for something that would alter my internal world enough to make me feel something different.

By age 16, I was a hit at the nightclubs, fueled by Cocaine and booze. By age 17, I was addicted to Crystal Meth. I had found my "something different" feeling; in fact, it was the best I had ever felt. My entire world began to revolve around my use, always chasing that initial feeling, which I never found again. I threw away any success I had built up for myself, regardless of how fleeting it was anyway. And I watched as everything I had worked so hard for - my passions, dreams, commitment, and years of tireless dedication - slip through my fingers like sand as I stood there paralyzed under the influence of the drug that became my Master. The grip that this drug had on me made it impossible for me to salvage any of what I had created for myself; real or imagined. I was a slave.

In the depths of my addiction, I willingly, yet somehow completely unknowingly, handed over mansions for slums, riches for shekels, and paradise for my own personal hell. As a broken and lost soul, I naturally surrounded myself with other broken and lost souls, a universal law. As a thirsty, lost, fatherless child seeking companionship and accolades that were no longer there, there was no other possibility but for me to be met by other lost individuals who might benefit from what they thought I had. I was an easy target with nothing to give, but plenty for others to steal. I had no choice but to sit back and watch my own carcass be picked clean, somehow sickly satisfied in my own victim mentality. I needed my drugs: meth, validation, and victimhood. I relished in the belief that I was the boy who would never be loved enough.

But you see, me and the parasites I attracted were the same. Like attracts like, hurt people hurt people, and sick people get other people sick. We had a symbiotic relationship. I needed people who looked, lived, and acted in ways that were as filthy and decrepit as I felt on the inside, and they needed a meal ticket and bragging rights. It just worked. Eventually the money ran out and I became more and more like the people I surrounded myself with. My holier than thou attitude no longer had a place, and it was met with vicious opposition and chaos. On numerous occasions, I was beaten to a pulp within an inch of my life - missing teeth, broken jaw, left for dead, hog-tied, kidnapped, shot at, guns in my mouth, you name it. And as I fought this battle with myself throughout the years, underneath my fictitious hardened exterior, I remained a small boy; I was afraid, confused, and lonely.

Unable to face the truth, I sank further and further into the abyss. I lived in stolen cars, other people's garages, and even settled for a friend's front patio. I was atrophied, eviscerated, and masticated. The pain was endless. I could feel the demons I unknowingly created out of my suppressed fears tearing at the threads of my existence. I fought harder, when I should have surrendered. And it became impossible to drown out the noise. I could feel creatures from the depths of hell pulling me into the darkest season of my life. It turned out, it was me pulling me all along. There was no hope for me and my then very small existence. There was no way out. I was stuck in the swirl of the toilet bowl of life, too deep to escape the flush.

On one particular day, not too unlike any other day I spent stuck in the flush of the bowl and in a drug-induced psychosis, I wept in the mirror while I mutilated my face. It was a habit I had gotten quite familiar with, a form of self-harm and self-soothing all in one. It gave me a sense of power, as if maybe I could remove the filth by incessantly clawing at my skin. Inflicting any amount of pain on the outside made me forget about the deep wounds I felt inside. And on this day, I was heartbroken over a girl I caught cheating on me; a fine example of a lower companion doing what hurt people do, and yet again I somehow believed that I was an exception to the rule, as I engaged in the same behaviors as her.

In a moment of clarity given to me by a power greater than myself, I was hurled out of my feverish ritual and observed myself in the mirror, bloodied and broken yet again. Deeply ashamed of where I was, and finally given some understanding that I needed help, I began recording myself with my phone. I did not want to lose this gift of desperation. I wanted to remember what it felt like to surrender. I earnestly spoke to myself, like the stern father I never had speaking to my inner child. I was harsh, direct, and clear. I spoke to myself through tears and bloodied cheeks. I begged myself to remember the pain and finally took accountability for my faults. It was time to let go. No mountain too high, no sacrifice too great, and no comforts to be clung to. If I was going to change anything, I had to change everything. And I couldn't do it alone.

I checked myself into a medical treatment facility for mental health and drug addiction. I had been to rehab many times over the years, with some success that ultimately ceased as a result of decisions I made based on self. This time was different. For the first time, I admitted complete defeat. Any other time I went, it was either to patch myself up a bit with no intent of making any lasting changes or to please or appease someone else. This time, I knew I needed to change everything for me and for everyone else around me. I was certain of my decision; I went immediately without stopping to tell anyone where I was going. Little did I know; I was about to embark on the most transformational journey I had ever been on. I had had years of sobriety before on multiple occasions, had done healing work, and even experienced breakthroughs with psychedelics. But what I experienced this time stretched far beyond any soft starts I had had in the past. Of course it did, it had to have. If I had known what I needed before on my own volition, I would have done it. This proved that my transformation had to come from something beyond my own limited perception and ideas of what healing should or could look like.

Because I finally entered this space with an open mind, without expectation, and without any attachment to my own ideas, I was empty enough to allow something bigger than me to grace me and pull me into the Kingdom of Heaven. There is an inspired teaching which states, "it is easier for a camel to go through the eye of a needle than for a rich person to enter the Kingdom of God." At that time, there was a narrow gate that one would need to pass through to enter Jerusalem. The people referred to this narrow opening as the "needle's eye." Before entering, the weary traveler would have to remove their belongings from their camels, get their camel onto all four knees, and inch the camel through this "needle's eye," leaving their belongings behind. That is to say; the more you own and attach to, regardless of its moral standing, the harder it is to let go and enter the Kingdom of Heaven. And to enter, you must let go. More profoundly, I have learned that the Kingdom of Heaven can be accessed right here right now. It is not some unattainable place that I may or may not enter once I leave my body. It is a state of mind, contingent upon my ability to let go of what I think I need, what I think I want, and what I think I know. When I entered rehab this time, for the last time, I was desperate and hopeless enough to have reached that place. As the saying goes, it is always darkest before the dawn, and how true that was for me in that moment.

The real work has come with my consistent surrender, as I am not always graced with that same desperation. Any moment I wish to enter the Kingdom of Heaven, I must let go all over again. I must become empty of me so that I may be graced with that same peace. The peace surpasses all understanding. Of course it does, it has to, because if I can understand it, that means it must come from me. And years of doing it my way have proven itself to be insufficient. I must repeatedly transcend me and transmit God, the Universe, or whatever you prefer to call it.

To maintain this state of mind, I had to take direction from others who had overcome the same struggles successfully and immerse myself in their mentorship. They guided me in exposing my ways of thinking and behaving that kept me sick, seeking refuge in something bigger (God), and sharing this process with others like they had done with me. I continue to engage in daily actions to ensure I will remain empty of me enough to stay free. Maintaining a practice with meditation and prayer, studying the teachings of spiritual leaders, surrounding myself with supportive relationships, developing discipline with physical fitness and a healthy diet, and above all prioritizing service to others are some of the actions I take to ensure spiritual expansion.

It is easy to drift away from the path by settling for familiar comforts or seeking temporary pleasures simply because it makes me feel good.

However, as I have seen on many occasions, this seemingly innocent and oftentimes societally encouraged behavior will eventually lead to another downward spiral. In this spiral, I miss the little, which costs me the much. The little refers to the subtle intricacies and delicacies that are the language of the universe conspiring in my favor, and they have been all along. Not only do I miss all that beauty, I cannot differentiate the true from the false; it is easy to convince myself that I am still on the path and that it is the world and its players who need to change. The self is cunning. It creeps back in when I least expect it. So, I must continue to engage in my daily practice. I must remain open and in a constant state of surrender.

Through continuous surrender in prayer, I experience the symphonic expression of the Divine - virtuous, wonderful, and powerful in Its ways. The irrevocably designed foundation and creation of this Universe, Universe, One Song, that exists within me and you and all around us, the Inner God we all possess. And somewhere along the way, I become the prayer, of course I do, I must. Because God exists within me, right here right now as the very life force energy coursing through my veins and woven into everything else all at the same time. This has been my awakening, my rebirth.

Coming into this awakening has also required absolute forgiveness of everyone and everything, and that I honor those who are hurting and blind, as I once was. Remember, I cannot remain free when I hold onto anything at all. So, I must recognize that we are no different, that Divine Principal works through us all the same, and that I must treat everyone as such. Otherwise I remain a slave, and once again my light dims. Today, I choose to remain a beacon of light and demonstrate these great spiritual Truths as a Soul Warrior. That is not to say that I don't fall short at times, but through prayer and meditation, I am righted in my tracks no matter how many times I fall short.

Again, the most important aspect of my life today, as a Soul Warrior, is sharing with others the Light I have found. No one is too dirty, too broken, or too far gone to find the Beauty of Life that sets us free. This state of being has allowed me, and can allow anyone, to become what I and my pack like to call… "unfuckwithable." No weapon formed against me shall prosper. Greater is that which is inside of me, than what I perceive to come against me in the outside world. Whatever is inside of me is what rules me. Today, I recognize that I have the Power to choose what I meditate on, what I give power to, and what I think and speak into existence. I have found that when I am quiet inside, I can access the inner room, the strength in the Secret Place to still my internal waters, as still waters best reflect the heavens. As one of the great metaphysical teachers I study speaks to, there is only one true problem on the face of this planet, and other than this one problem, no other exists. This singular problem we all share as human beings is our ability to rise above what we believe to be a problem, our ability to see the Truth. The only way to rise above is on a tide of spirituality, with love, compassion, understanding, and a willingness to let go of whatever it is I think I know.

I can finally see that my greatest life achievements have had nothing to do with fame. True success can only be experienced in the present moment. And in a successful series of right here, right nows - I am willing to become open to everything and attached to nothing, with a heavy focus on how I can serve others. I have found fulfillment in any moment I am able to maintain that state of Being. Don't wait like I did. This moment - right here, right now - could be the very moment in your life that you awaken to who you truly are and what you are truly capable of, as a Spiritual Being having a human experience, a Soul Warrior.

JEREMY JACKSON

Actor / Producer / Transformative Breathwork Practitioner / Sober Coach / Personal Wellness Coach

Connect: jeremyjacksonfitness.com / @jeremyjacksonfitness

ERIK THURESON
SYMPHONY OF HOPE: A FATHER'S TALE OF FINDING STRENGTH THROUGH SUFFERING

A notification chimes in the dark. A few seconds later, her phone chimes. Neither of them pick up to check the messages, after all it is three am and both of them are fast asleep. It was a start to another hot summer day here in Arizona. I rolled out of bed, stepped into a very intentional cold shower to fully wake up. After the normal routine of brushing the teeth, getting dressed and meditation, I finally noticed the text. It was from Jacob, *love you dad* with a time stamp of 3:19am. I text him back, *love you too, have a great day.* It was a little after 8am. I figured he was up late as usual recording. He was a recording artist signed to Atlantic Records at age seventeen the previous fall. I didn't expect him to reply as he was most likely asleep from being up all night in the studio. That seemed to be his usual routine considering he lived a few short blocks from the studio.

Making my morning coffee and getting ready to walk out the door for work, Judy sat at the kitchen table writing and planning her next retreat and client coaching group. She expressed her concern of something bad possibly happening to Jacob. It was a pattern or coincidence that when she started doing or planning something great for her business, something would happen to Jacob. As far as she was concerned, this was the pattern and it worried her. The aroma of fresh brewed coffee filled the kitchen. I turned to her and said confidently, 'Not this time, you will create something great.' As I grabbed my coffee and my bag to head out the door for work, her phone rang. I paused to see who it might be, she mouthed 'Evelyn'. That was Jacob's girlfriend. We had just spent the previous weekend in Los Angeles together with her, Jacob and our daughters Emma and Sydney. It was a great time of go karts, tacos, City Walk, visiting him in the studio and sandwiches from Fat Sals. Surprisingly, even the traffic was light and breezy. I was still on a high from what a great time we had together with everyone. Jacob was doing well, seemingly healthy, happy, and he was initiating and present. So out the door I went off to work for what I thought was just another regular Thursday.

As I arrived at work, I received a series of texts and missed calls. Judy was frantically trying to reach me. *What? I just saw her twenty minutes ago?! What happened? What's going on?* I settle into the office, and then call her back. *Apparently* Jacob was being rushed to the emergency room. She was a bit hysterical as she could not get a clear diagnosis or report as to what his condition was. Apparently it was the doctor's and hospital's policy to not give specific or detailed information out over the phone. I asked for the contact information and said I would get some answers. We were six hours away, in Phoenix, and he was in Hollywood. I assured her I would get some answers. I wasn't panicked, you see this wasn't the first time we had been here. Jacob being taken to the ER, that is.

Let's rewind the clock back a few years, back to a time when we lived in Austin, Texas. This is where this journey, or should I say discovery of, began. We discovered Jacob smoking pot at fourteen. We had a talk, and he assured us it wasn't a problem and he was just curious. It didn't seem to continue to our knowledge, so we left it at that. It wasn't until he started displaying some erratic behaviour that we became concerned. With a little investigation, we discovered a considerable amount of pills that he had apparently got off the dark web. It turned out to be Xanax and Molly as we later discovered after taking him to the ER for the first time. We had no idea what it was and didn't want to take any chances. He was there overnight, sobered up and came home the next day. That is what sent us on the path of discovery and recovery. Therapists, counsellors, psychologists, psychiatrists and a slew of doctors visits resulted in a clinical diagnosis of depression and anxiety. The medication he was prescribed according to him was only making him feel worse. After a number of different medically supervised medications and treatments failed, he took matters into his own hands, and this is where the trouble really began. However, at sixteen, he started making good progress with the last counsellor and outpatient program he attended. The day before he was scheduled to graduate from the program, there was an episode where another kid at the meeting gave him something. Later that night at three in the morning, I heard voices coming from his room. He was clearly out of his right mind and talking nonsense. Judy calls the paramedics, and being a sleepy town, five sheriffs show up with the paramedics. His heart rate was north of 185 beats per minute and needed to be sedated and stabilised. Three of the officers had to hold him down in the middle of my living room so the EMT could give him the sedative. And off he went, yet again to the ER. That time he went to an inpatient program but that is a whole other story. Back to the present situation.

So rather than let my imagination run wild and stress out, I was unusually calm seeking to understand what the details were. *Did we need to drop everything and get to California? Or was this another 'episode'?* After a couple of attempts to get through all the message prompts, I finally got the doctor on the phone. He shared some general details and that he was on a respirator, stable, but in a comatose state not responding to external commands or stimulus. He also stated we should come as soon as possible. We hang up. I sat in my office in a state of shock. What happened? How did we get here? What's going on? Am I dreaming? Is this really happening right now? This was not like the times before.

Still in shock, I talked with my supervisor to let him know what was happening. In full support, he said I needed to go and be with Jacob and the family and not to worry about work and it would be covered. That is when it really started to sink in. He gave me a hug and some encouraging words as my heart sank to the floor. Making arrangements to get a flight, car and place to stay would have taken just as long or longer than jumping in the car and making the six-hour drive to Los Angeles, so that's what we did. It was the longest drive and seemed like forever to get there. It was silent. We sat with our thoughts and feelings as the dry, desert, cactus-lined miles went by. How bad is he? Will he be okay, knowing that when doctors say 'you should be here' isn't usually a good thing. After a very quiet, yet agonising, drive due to the uncertainty and all the feels, we finally arrive at the Hollywood Presbyterian Medical Center where Jacob had been admitted.

It was early evening, 13 June as we pulled into the parking structure. Tired and hungry, but too concerned about our boy, we made our way up to the ICU on the fourth floor. My hope was walking in that during the time it took us to get there, his condition would have improved and he would be awake. That was wishful thinking and sadly wasn't the case. It was cold, the intercom was active with calls over the loudspeakers, the smell of disinfectant filled the air. It was clean, but not a warm welcoming clean like you would feel at home, more of a sterile clean. As you would expect, he was pretty messed up, not a sight you would ever want to see your child in. He was also shivering from the hyperthermic treatment they had him on. My son, Jacob, my little buddy, isn't okay. He was pale. He is hanging on by a thread and dependent on these machines and medication to keep him alive. He can't tell me how he is feeling. He can't acknowledge that he knows we are here. My heart was being pummelled and shattered into a million little pieces at each passing moment. *How did this happen? Why did this happen? What happened? God where were you when my little boy needed help?* This is hard to write as the tears are welling up as I relive this story. It was and is my worst nightmare, as you can imagine. No parent should ever go through seeing their child like this. It isn't how this is supposed to work. Our children are supposed to bury us not the other way around. After a long, excruciating day in the ICU, we retreated back to the hotel a few blocks away for some much-needed rest.

Early the next morning, before anyone else was up, I rolled out of bed straight to the floor on my knees and prayed the single most difficult prayer of my life. 'God, you know what I want. Jacob to wake up and walk out of this place. However, if it would be for the greater good, though I don't understand how or why, that you take him now, then so be it.' With tears in my eyes, I got up and got ready for another long day in the ICU. I wasn't at peace. I wasn't resolved. I was still wrestling with holding tightly to the outcome I wanted. The atmosphere was heavy, dark and seemingly hopeless. I did my best to be present, to learn all the things, and share with Jacob what was happening as we fully believed he could hear everything that was going on. We played music, shared stories and held tightly to the hope that he would pull through. There were tests, medications, brain scans, hypothermic treatment to increase the odds of recovery. Friends, family, producers and other music artists poured into the tiny room one after another all throughout the day and evening. The EEG brain scans were inconclusive, an apnea breathing test would be attempted the next day. One of the medical specialists pulled me aside to ask about organ donation, and I glared at him and said sternly, 'Yeah, he's gonna need those! Are you serious right now?' Clearly after a day and half we are not talking about this.

An apnea test was planned for two reasons. The first, of which I was aware of, was to see if he could breathe on his own and sustain a sufficient oxygen level in his blood. The second of which was a brain test, which I was unaware of, to see if the part of his brain that controls his breathing was damaged. No-one knows exactly how long he had stopped breathing for or how long he was without oxygen.

The next day, I followed the same routine, praying, saying the same thing, 'God, you know what I want, but if it is for the greater good and will glorify you more that you take him, so be it.' And right back to the ICU we went with anxious anticipation of the looming tests. I still was not surrendered, nor was I letting go. This is my little buddy we are talking about, my son, my firstborn. When you are in the midst of a traumatic event like this, I noticed a heightened sense of focus, attention to detail, a sensitivity to the environment seen and unseen. I knew all the medical staff, nurses, specialists and the host of doctors that had any influence over Jacob's care. I learned their routines, what treatments were for what, medications and even what was going on with some of the other patients from their families in the lobby.

This was another dark and heavy day. The atmosphere was thick and palpable. During the test, I assisted the respiratory technician for the apnea test. We removed the respirator. He needed to breathe on his own with an acceptable sustained oxygen level for five minutes. I was glued to the timer, no-one else was allowed in the room. It was just the three of us. Thirty seconds ... forty-five ... one minute. Whispering to Jacob, 'You got this, buddy. Keep going!' A minute fifteen ... Justin, the technician, checking his blood gas levels, had a disappointed look. My face fell, my heart sank and tears welled up. His blood oxygen had started falling ninety-six ... ninety-four ... ninety-one ... eighty-eight. He could not breathe well enough to sustain the oxygen levels he needed. We had to abort the test. I was emotionally drained from what seemed like hours yet only seconds. And what did that mean exactly.

The neurologist and the ER physician that initially treated him when he arrived both spoke with us that evening at different times. The ER doctor said that was a miracle that we were even here and that he was still with us considering his dismal condition upon arrival. She stated he was in extremely bad shape and again it was miraculous that we were having this conversation at this point. All that said, she wasn't positive in any way, other than she was positive it wasn't going to end well. There was a darkness around her and the energy I was feeling from her wasn't good and it wasn't about the news she was giving us. It was how she was giving it. It was a few hours sitting with this news and the heaviness of the test failure was weighing us down.

The neurologist came by and said that they would try the apnea test again the next day. Jacob was stable from a stressful day and needed rest. He also mentioned that if he fails the test again that we would need to start planning for final arrangements. He too was cold, matter of fact and seemingly without feeling on the matter. Hard. Calloused. Which I imagine is to be expected if you are dealing with death and dying people for the last twenty-two years. It was an emotional roller-coaster and darkness started to envelop what little hope we had left. Exhausted, we retreated back to the hotel, arriving shortly after 2am.

I didn't sleep much, though my physical body needed it. My mind and heart were not okay. Some hours later, I rolled out of bed, straight to the floor. On my knees before God for the third day, saying the same thing. Today was different, I had a vision as I prayed.

It was dark, pitch black, with a single spotlight cascading a bright white light down on a black stage from upper left to a widening lower right. There was what seemed to be gold dust floating in the air. It wasn't moving in any particular direction, just around. It was peaceful. Then the vision faded to black as if to wrap the end of a movie scene. As I got up, a calm wave of peace that transcends all understanding washed over me all at once. I stood there, in amazement of how I was feeling despite the challenges that the day would bring. Here I was, present, peaceful, surrendered. The outcome didn't matter, I had no control over that. It was in God's hands, and I trusted He knew what was best. I was in His hands too. He had me. I had Him. The fact that I would be facing the darkest Father's Day was about to unfold, yet I had peace. A confidence that no matter what the outcome, it would be for the greater good. I became completely unattached to the specificity of my will and the outcome I desired. I was ready to face whatever challenge this day had to throw at me.

Another apnea test was on the schedule. You could practically chew on the air in the room, it was so thick. The atmosphere was still, sterile and hopeless. The grief mounted as the clock ticked and the minutes wore on as the looming test approached. Another thing I learned while in the ICU was that the great state of California reserves the right to pull the plug on patients without consent if the physician in charge of the patient's care reports that the patient is in fact brain dead to avoid prolonged and unnecessary life support. Armed with this information, I avoided getting direct reports regarding Jacob's brain health from the primary physician. I got it from all the other sources, technicians, specialists and nurses.

On this particular morning, I heard a physician out in the hall going over the cases and their respective course of care. I peeked out from behind the door to listen in on his report for Jacob and what treatment he would be getting. He and the nursing staff were circled up, taking notes, mid-discussion as the doctor noticed me peeking out from behind the door. 'Can I help you?' he asked. I replied, 'No, don't mind me. I don't want to interrupt. Carry on,' in hopes that he would do just that. I would not be so lucky. He abruptly halted their meeting as they all looked at me as I began to shrink in stature. 'Are you Jacob's dad?' he asked. 'Yes, yes I am,' I replied as my heart started beating out of my chest. He continued, 'I understand he is scheduled to do another breathing test today, that he failed yesterday. Well, we aren't doing that. He is young, only eighteen, and can possibly bounce back from this. I cannot make any promises, but we need to give him more time. So that is exactly what we are going to do, give him more time.' I nodded in agreement, and barely got a whispered 'thank you' out before bursting into tears heading back into the room. I slumped down into the chair, out of breath, crying uncontrollably. Judy, and the girls, started crying because I was crying but didn't know what had just happened. I couldn't talk, trying to catch my breath and gain my composure, I sat there for about five minutes. I was overwhelmed with hope and joy that Jacob would have the time he needed and this doctor that I hadn't seen before was the deliverer of that hope. I finally got the words out and shared what had just transpired out in the hall. More tears, but the atmosphere shifted. It was lighter, the despair had left, and it was replaced with hope. It was as tangible as storm clouds parting as the rays of light broke through.

As I sat there taking in all that had just happened, I realised I did not get the doctor's name. I jump up out the door only to discover that he is gone. I walk over to the nurse's desk and ask, 'Who was the physician that was just here?' The nurse replied, 'Oh, that was Dr Emmanuel.' As I headed back into the room, realising what the name Emmanuel means, I burst into an even uglier cry slumping back into the chair. 'Now what?!' Judy says to me. Again, I am unable to speak for another five minutes. Moments later, I finally eek out the works, 'His name is Dr Emmanuel.' She teared up as she realized his name means 'God is with us' and says, 'Of course. Of course it is.'

We spent the next eleven days with Jacob, friends, family, pastors, artists, producers, sharing stories, songs, music, singing and making the most of the time we had. I found Dr Emmanuel on day twelve in the hall getting ready to go into another patient's surgery. I told him, 'Thank you. I remember you said you couldn't make any promises and things aren't looking good. However, I wanted to express my gratitude for you and giving us this time with him. Had it not been for your intervention, we might not have had this. For that I will always be grateful. Thank you.' And gave him a God-size hug, knowing he did everything he could to give Jacob what he and all of us needed. Time.

It was exactly two weeks. Two weeks from the day he was admitted to the day he passed, 27 June 2019 at 5:11am. Just a few short hours before, he had cardiac arrest, coded and was given CPR. It was time. He was ready. His body tired of all the fighting. I whispered in his ear, 'It's okay, little buddy. We'll be okay. I love you, I forgive you. And it's okay, you're free to go if you want to.' As the staff looked at me for permission to stop further attempts to resuscitate him in the event of another code, I calmly looked around the room. It was as if time itself stopped and honoured this boy, this young man. Everything at that moment felt like slow motion. My focus was clearer than it had ever been, my spirit more present than I had ever felt. It was a very intense moment. Judy curled on the floor crying and screaming as Emma tried to comfort her. I said, 'No more.' They faded away from his bed, as our family gathered around him. I stood to his right, holding his right hand with my left, and placing my right hand on his chest. We watched his heart rate slow in his final moments, as tears rolled down our faces, we prayed. I felt his final heartbeat in my hand. Through the tears and shortness of my breath, I prayed and committed his spirit into God's hands. The rest of that morning was a bit of a blur. I do recall wanting to be the one to communicate with the next shift of nurses what had happened as we all became pretty close in the two weeks we were there. More tears and hugs. Then I think we passed out from all of it for a few days.

It was during this time that God said to me through the Spirit one simple phrase that I will carry on as long as I am still breathing and that was this, 'Steward your suffering well.' Unclear what that meant in the moment, I was completely clear however on the words. He mentioned it a few more times that first week as we retreated to Ames Lake, Washington, with family to decompress and grieve in the peaceful setting of summer in the Pacific Northwest. We spent five days there. The weather was perfect, the mountain air was clean. The lake was still like glass. I spent time meditating. I also paddleboarded a few times. It was so surreal as the lake reflected the scattered clouds perfectly and it felt like

I was paddleboarding in the heavens. I spent time crying and grieving as well.

Steward your suffering well. What did that mean exactly? I meditated on this phrase for the coming weeks. I met with a close friend, Jay Salazar, who had also lost his son Zach in a similar fashion just a year earlier. He had no idea what I had just gone through when I asked to meet up for dinner. We didn't live in the same state. We hadn't seen each other in quite a few years. Yet he could tell the seriousness in the request, and like a true friend and brother agreed. We talked into the early hours of the morning, brothers of a fraternity that no-one pledges nor would care to join under any circumstances. Yet, here we were.

It dawned on me during our conversation a few important things. One, God knew exactly how I felt. Two, he puts people in our lives that have suffered similar things to walk with us during the suffering. And lastly, what steward my suffering well meant. It meant I needed to share this suffering with others in the same way Jay showed up for me. After spending time with him, I believed unswervingly he knew exactly what I was going through and how I felt. I knew I could carry on. He already proved and demonstrated that example for me. You see, just at the right time, we suffer, so that when others suffer we can meet their needs. My suffering is not just for me. I am called to lean into this story, share it openly, and by doing so, it will help someone else.

Jacob was a light that burned twice as bright yet half as long. He was not a drug addict. He did not suffer from poor moral character. He wasn't destitute nor desperate. He struggled with his mental health and his faith in a medical system that failed him. We took every step, gave him every resource, and left no stone unturned for him to get the care he needed. Like many eighteen-year-olds, he thought he knew better. He thought there was a better way. This was not the outcome any of us wanted. But he was right. There is a better way. The encouragement knowing there is a greater purpose to this suffering makes it a little bit easier to do, reliving this grief, this trauma, this tragedy. Jacob has hundreds of thousands of fans across the globe. Judy and I have and will continue to openly love and support any and all of the Cupid Soldiers. In the last four years since his passing, we have encouraged dozens of teens and young adults to get sober. Additionally, we have also talked quite a few more out of suicide and saw to it that they have received the help that they desperately needed. This is what steward your suffering well means. This is the better way. Leaning into difficult discussions as parents, removing any moral condemnation or high ground, and providing a safe environment without shame, guilt or judgement. Showing up with unfailing love, unswerving compassion and uncompromising kindness, this is the better way.

ERIK THURESON
Filmmaker / Producer / Creator
Connect: @erikthureson

RHIANNON PARKER
LETTING GO OF EMILY

My story is not a yarn or made-for-television docudrama that has an epic tale. Neither is it a 'once upon a time' story, although it may be the only way to explain to give you a visual of the visceral experience and the clever plots that by a mind trying to protect, create safety and live into programmed behaviour after a serious mind-melding trauma.

This narration is my truism – a mix of gut-wrenching horror followed by kaleidoscopic turns and twists. A sharing from an ordinary woman of extraordinary resilience and bravery who overcomes a life-threatening experience facilitated by a lifelong commitment of care to heal and become whole again.

Let us discuss the characters, myself – Rhiannon – a gang of guys, my friends and lastly, Emily. Emily plays both antagonist and protagonist in a cruel and loving way throughout this dialogue. Emily was my way of surviving a horrific, gruelling, hellacious, unrelenting and unforgiving night of terror that no woman, let alone human being, should bear. She is the epitaph so that I could survive and move through the agony from the inside out. Later, we will talk about how I was not surviving, I was gently pulling myself apart one praise, purge, exercise and hiding from life at a time.

Let us set the scene. It was a time of celebration and achievement, coming into adulthood where the comradery of friends meets the road of anticipated youthful frolic. We all look to that day when we graduated high school and came into our own, and I was no exception. I was living my best moment. On a night designed to have fun in the form of going out and tasting the sweet libation of alcoholic drinks, dancing and being with my mates, it started to turn sour when suddenly without warning, as the crowd moved, I find myself swept off my feet and knocked to the dance floor. Amid hundreds of raging people, I shakily stood up, hoping, as I became upright, that my friends were there waiting.

In the middle of that club, I was alone, separated from them. All that remained was a buzz of loud, so loud I could not hear myself think, a lone fish in a pool of people. Disconnected from my support, my friends, the people who kept me safe, I was on the verge of tears, trying so hard to be brave. Being brave, I have learned, sometimes means we get to be vulnerable with ourselves, speaking your truth in that second, coupling with the emotion that arrives. My truth at that minute – my friends were nowhere. We always had a safety plan, to meet outside the women's bathroom as a gathering point. I went to that place and waited, watching minutes tick by, one after the other. Suddenly I felt even more alone, vulnerable.

Warmed with alcohol, a quicksand sensation rose from the inside out and I had to do something besides panic. Instincts kicked in as I pushed my way through those swarms of bodies, in a concrete sardine can. I soon discovered my friends had disappeared into this abyss and technology could not save me. No reception.

Leaving the dance, the swarm, I headed to the women's bathroom one more time before searching for the closest exit. Having been unsuccessful at reuniting with my friends, my goal was to commandeer cell reception to see if I had missed any calls. As I made my way to the street-level room, I stopped and asked the hosts for help, who suggested going outside the club. Heading toward a door to find the bouncer, the guardian of the masses, I thought he may know something of my mystery and help me unfold added information.

It was hard to keep myself together, as the emotional pressure welled up inside my soul, heart and mind magnified by the alcohol. The mystic spell that numbs your senses and exacerbates, heightens your emotions. Reaching the bouncer, the equivalent of a wood cutter like in Snow White, I found solace. Amongst the noise and dozens upon dozens of people and my detailed descriptions, although I was warm with alcohol, he was able to give me directions and assurance as to their whereabouts.

The plot in this story is about to take a twist. A twist that is very real, not imagined or made up. It is life-changing, soul-tarnishing in the worst kind of way and depraved. Innocence stolen, trust in feeling safe demolished, hope demoralised and survival is the new queen.

Anxious and uncertain, spending frantic moments in tears when I left the club in desperation.

I walked through the streets one block after the other following the bouncers' directions, losing count as I wandered past endless streets hoping to find my friends. My soul was cringing at the thought that I may never find my friends, this hope and truth stuck with me like super glue throughout my ordeal.

Despite the effects of alcohol, my inner compass enabled me to orient myself with the surroundings outside the club. I was aware – aware when the crowds stopped, and I was completely alone. In this state of being, I faced unknown and known circumstances. I vaguely recall I thought they – my friends – may have been hungry and went to get something to eat. That sounded logical to me. I headed towards the left, crossed a street and could see the KFC and Macca's up on the left under dim streetlights. Finally arriving, I looked in hurriedly, but could not see them, so I kept walking.

Ahead of me crossing the road, I noticed there were five men standing outside a shop front drinking, talking and smoking. I was alone, completely alone ... I had to figure out a plan immediately on getting past them as quickly as possible. Head down, no eye contact, walking briskly and saying nothing. There was no immediate choice but to get around it. No safe avenues or alternatives were accessible – it was a busy street and trams were coming and going down the middle of the road and nowhere to cross. It was like a scene in the movie where you walk into a cave, choose a path then reach a dead end and to get through you must take the path where the spider web is.

I now feel unsafe. Soon those feelings became like a spidery sixth sense, a sick feeling in my throat and tummy – this was not good. The words that come to mind that describe my feelings at the time were unsafe, terrified, sick, uneasy, intuitive instincts to protect, small, vulnerable and my deep to my soul truth, *I am not going to get out of this.*

The villains – salacious, determined, angry, a hypervigilant unrelenting antagonist who ruled with an iron fist to get his will met. As I followed my plan to walk quickly past this group of men, where I had no other choice, I said nothing and kept my eye on the goal. Almost reaching the end of my goal, as I whipped like the wind past the final man, a surge of heat, strength and overpowering fell upon me. His breath bathed in alcohol and a giant hand around me, pulling, tugging, I tried all I could to pull away from his vice grip. I wrestled with a man with a resolve to get his way. Uncertain what that meant, we played a game of body tug of war.

In a drunken state, the first invasion of my personal space began. In garbled tones, I heard, 'Girl, why don't you give me a kiss!' This inebriated male took it upon himself to force his lips on mine. His rancid breath and overwhelming disdain for women was very present. His large manly hands grabbed my arm as I walked by, the echo of, 'Girl, what are you doing here!'

It was repulsive and disgusting, taking all the strength I had to repel his physical overtures. I stood my ground and in protest, slapped his face, letting him know that I was not that kind of woman. Covered in the drench of his unwelcomed affections, all I could do to was to put into action a love of sports and make a mad dash. With light-footed speed I ran and ran and ran. As fast as I could, I ran, telling myself with each step I was going to get out of this.

I tried to outrun them, in my wedges which in turn broke abruptly at the pace I was travelling. My handbag dropped as I swiftly took flight to fling my shoes off with eagerness so I could continue toward safety. In seconds, I realised as I scanned ahead and looked behind me, they were all on my trail. Hot on my path were five men with an attitude of barbaric misdoing, eager to breach the freedom and rights of another.

I moved quickly through the gray shadows of buildings and dimmed lights. As I turned into an alleyway, I realised that my mad dash was about to come to a mad halt. A dead end; this was truly life exemplifying art. You know the part in the movie when there is nowhere to go? My heart was racing frantically, and I thought to myself, *What is he going to do with me?* I knew I was about to face a nightmare, even lose my life. What a dreadful heart-pumping, end-of-mortality-driven scene. Scanning the area, I tried to figure out where to go next. They were getting closer, and my time was running out.

The pace and sounds in this life-movie changed rapidly, the sounds of large running footsteps in-between yelling of vulgar expletives that make your stomach churn in disdain. I scaled a wire fence in bare feet only to feel a large hand jerk me back down, down, down. Landing on the ground with a large thud, meeting the very menacing face of a man enraged, drunk and ready like a scorpion to strike – and he did, with a vicious sting.

I am going to press pause and yell, *CUT!* Creative license allows such a moment because with the deepest of reverence may I say, we all know what is about to happen. I have set a menacing gut-check scene. This is where with compassion and love I say that not all details need a voice of the spoken word. Those of you reading this who may be grasping at straws to heal and deal with your own life-changing experiences need the same understanding.

On that note what I can say of that night is this: one after the other, the onslaught of assaults continued into that dark night. I have small recollections of images that do not make sense even when I try to put the pieces together. Eventually, there was nothingness to which I have surmised was my unconscious state. Left like a ragdoll, human garbage I lay there with no fight left, bruised, cut, broken and alone. Hours would have passed by without me knowing, or anyone else for that matter, I later discovered.

THE RIDE HOME ...

Dawn had arrived at the horizon, as the sun skirted across my face and streetlights were off and all was quiet. I had regained consciousness. Everything hurts. My head was throbbing, my throat felt like I had swallowed razor blades. I put my hand to the back of my head and I could feel a large bump. I asked myself over and over if this a bad dream. Glancing down at my clothes, the jagged cuts, now looking like crusted bulges of blood, sprawled on the concrete, I dragged myself up. Feeling wobbly and shaken, in tremendous pain, in a daze I tried to piece things together. Quickly scattered mental images and recollections of the night before haunted my mind.

Those images affirmed this ordeal was not a bad dream but every bit real. The telltale signs of a serious struggle had occurred. I immediately felt embarrassed and exposed, so I took some time to compose myself in a way that was less demeaning. I eventually got myself to my feet, nearly losing my balance as I stood. I keeled over and vomited. Upright, I methodically walked toward the last known place of my personal effects down the alleyway. In the distance as I walked, I noticed my handbag, phone and shoes were untouched, still in the same place I had left them hours before.

I checked my phone – nothing, not one text or call. Empty, I put my handbag over my shoulder, grabbed my shoes mechanically and walked toward the main road. Feeling disoriented, my entire body ached beyond measure, slowly plodding along, the only sense I had after realising that none – not one – of my friends checked in on me or my whereabouts was to take the train. Confused, trying to make sense of it all, the only singular thought was to get home, it felt safer, my refuge from this. This rage of another that now felt shamed, afraid and unwilling to express what had happened. *What if* loomed at every juncture, my mind a mess of images, and luckily, the logic amidst all the mess, arrived. Take the train home.

My head hurt; all was a fog with glimpses of light flashing through my mind. The loud noises, the repeated hurt, followed by excruciating pain. Like a robot or under a spell I moved forward, unaware of anyone, I just wanted to be alone. Curl up into a ball and disappear at home. The thought of home brought pangs of emotion. Getting home was my goal now.

There is not much that I can tell you about that ride home, it was all a blur like a fast-speeding train running through your mind. Getting off the train at Lilydale, I had enough cognitive ability to plan the walk home through Warby Trail. Barefoot, hurt, alone, ready to burst, I felt nothing. I was numb, shutting down every emotion just like a robot walking home with dogmatic determination.

HOME ... A SANCTUARY

The safety of home had arrived, and even as numb as I was, I welcomed it. Brushing my teeth seemed like a good step in finding myself in the aftermath. I crawled into the shower, knowing I had my clothes on, and it did not seem to matter. What mattered was convincing myself to take off that guilt-ridden and shame-drenched clothes. I could not, I would not. Facing myself was the worst pain to bear, far greater than any physical.

Constant gnawing at my soul, the thought battle of whether to BE not to BE, that is the question … in Shakespearean terms. My similitude was much more physically based – to clothe or not to clothe that was the dilemma facing me with each drip of the shower, rhythmically pelting my aching, damaged body.

All I could do was stand there, warm water dripping endlessly over my bruised and battered body, alone in my pain, paralysed. The cuts burned and yet being emotionally numb it did not seem to matter. What did matter – the clock ticked by loudly and the internal battle raged. Bursting into tears, I let go; it was too much, whimpering quietly, curled up in that shower, my inner little girl tried to help me find solace and comfort despite being stricken with the paralysing feeling that perhaps at any moment, the terror would return, I clung to myself, my body convulsed with vomit at the very thought.

Time seemed to stand still as I peeled the layers of clothing from my skin. The warmth of the shower and being at home eventually brought a morsel of relief. Fresh courage and strength slowly surfaced as I worked through taking care of myself. Adorned in PJs, I reached for my phone, to see if there was a glimpse, just a small one of any of my friends. Anger found my hand as I hurled my phone at my window – nothing. I flopped my hurt body onto the bed and sunk into the abyss of tears. It was agonising to know there was no text or phone call, ever greater the realisation that I could not tell a soul. What would they think of me, and in that moment, I was demonising myself as the worst person on the earth All I could do was cry, cry so much with pain and shame that I fell asleep.

NEW NORMAL – THE PATH TO HEALING

Upon the dawn of the days that followed, my determination surfaced around the decisions and commitment that I made to myself. My decisions were hallmarks around how I was to cope or find a new normal. All those years ago, healing was not even a thought in the immediate aftermath. Ensuring that my secret died with me was.

Now my life mission was to protect myself at all costs. Protect myself so that I would not experience such terror again and hide from the truth that meant my family and friends would, if they knew, heavily judge me. Judge me in a way that is scathing, unloving and point the finger, blame me for what transpired. At all costs, even my own personal growth, I could not breach this covenant I made with myself.

This oath of allegiance meant it was time to go to work to get myself in tip-top condition. After all, when you are on such a mission, controlling every aspect of your life determines the outcomes you are looking for. I was looking for a facade that would be a measure that nothing was wrong and that I was okay. A facade that would take on an enormous part of my life, not only then, but even to this very day.

Imagine if you want to bury a secret so terrible. What do you think your soul, heart, mind does to achieve it? Our minds are a marvellous tool that can, if not controlled, put you on a path that feels safe, however in truth is a barbed trail strewn with debris of unhealing, unhealthy coping skills and survival mechanisms that drive the bus of life. I decided to pack up my secret in layers of boxes, wrapped in chains and padlocks and put it away, never recovered for the rest of my life. Only that was a survival mechanism so that I could control life and life could not control me.

Life from the inside out was tantamount to my inner compass taking refuge, creating mutiny and it looked like the mirror in *Snow White,* when the queen asks who is the fairest in the land. This internal compass facilitated messages and commands to ensure I could feel safe, certain, protected and protect me from any further hurt. Those implemented plans were based on the reflection of my research to follow a strict program like those of celebrities to be at a peak fitness level, weight and physical appearance.

'Mirror, mirror' was an eternal cauldron of cackling, toil and not enough. A central hub of dialog, twenty-four seven operations streaming to my subconscious where the hurt lay buried. At each turn, there were reminders, memorandums, gilded guilt trips and quick-witted intentions delivered hastily without compunction to ensure maximum results to unrelenting standards.

Payment and price for such an undertaking was a mere acknowledgement of my achievement, only to fall short, not being enough, unable to achieve. I recall that this state of mind severed any semblance of worthiness I may have felt. My mindset bowed stoically at every movement. Remember earlier in this narration, we touched on how I was not surviving, I was gently pulling myself apart through praise, purge, exercise and hiding from life.

What is important to understand for victims of violent crimes, life changes quickly. To get past the pain, there were moments of minimisation, that 'everything is fine'. Often mentally I went into an underground mode, pretending as if nothing happened, that by acting this way it would dissociate from the insidious events, returning life back to before the assault. Despite such a bold move, at least I thought emotional issues remained unchecked, unhealed.

My world had become a threatening place, where my hypervigilance, startle response and persistent fear engulfed my life constantly. Reluctance to go places for me was like living in a third dimension. I would only leave to meet the strict and rigid gym and sporting activities needed to ensure my physical appearance was of star quality. Every day felt like a walking nightmare. Let me paint a picture – think of a scene where you step into an alternate universe, a 'twilight zone' in the architecture of the landscape, the ground covered in mists of darkness created an eerie sentiment, making my skin crawl. Yet despite those things, I was still convinced I was okay.

Socialisation removal intact, for two years I lived like a hobbit under the command of a *Harry Potter* dementor, who in time sucked the very life out of me. After several years of therapy, I would name her Emily. You see, Emily was my dis-ease, my control to bear the burden of that padlock chained secret I had been carrying around, like a large boulder. The dis-ease was anorexia nervosa, a careful, stealthy illness that was a coping means to deal with my assault disorder hidden beneath the 'I'm okay'.

Emily, occupied with vengeance 'mirror, mirror' command and would strategically lift me up only to tear me down if I did not follow her guidelines, rules and goals with exactness. There was a constant five alarm war in my head. Shortening the war, of negative meant that my voice be louder and stronger than the influence of Emily's. Unfortunately, I was not at a place in my healing path to know how to silence, avoid, disperse this BITCH – Brilliant Internal Technique Calculating Hinderance aka anorexia nervosa. The price was high, higher than I had ever thought, and it was taking its toll. I was afraid to stop the barrage of her voice and did not know how to.

What I do know is that the duration of pain was significant. It added up to 730 which spanned two years. Finally, like all experiences we have, there is a decisive moment. Remember the scene in *Harry Potter* where Luna and Harry were the only ones who could see the vestrals. As you know, if you are an astute *Harry Potter* knower, vestals are only visible to those who have seen death or had a near-death experience in life. While at dinner with my family, I was exceptionally nervous, which for me was not unusual. However, for my family it was most unexpected. With this heightened sense of awareness, a disruption showed up to exacerbate my already unstable sensibilities. The disruption was an image of a stranger who fit close to the description of one of the assailants who assaulted me two years ago. That was the vestral in the night with darkened winged flight, the so-called image of a man, a stranger who almost looked like my rapist, a night I spiritually, emotionally lost Rhiannon.

His image flashed like a large firecracker going off and my panic set in rapidly. Agitated, unnerved, I snapped and rambled incoherently that it was time to go, and we had to leave now. Wanting not to disturb the family gathering too much, my mother took the lead and brought me home.

Upon arriving at home, my safe place, my mum, growing increasingly concerned, questioned my behaviours nervously. Words crossed the air like fiery darts. Emotions heightened and in a burst of emotion, I blurted out my story. I broke my covenant, and there in the middle of my bedroom, my mother fell to the floor like a puddle of clothes – lifeless. Her pain at my confession was visible, if only my words did not hurt so much. This was my start to healing and recovery.

The path to healing is one filled with pitfalls and obstacles. I went from pillar to post for psychiatric eating disorder treatment to another, unable to find the care that would bring me to let go of the boulder I was dragging around. The dis-ease needed trust. An expectation that would challenge my thinking and build a haven of faith where 'mirror, mirror' central – Emily's realm – would unfold naturally without resistance. I am grateful that I did not give up and found someone who would not give up on me, the Rhiannon version, not the Emily perspective. Relinquishing came when I found a health care provider who brought an approach my heart could feel.

Effects of certain life experiences can plague us deeply. Acceptance has been key to my journey to recovery. I know that Emily is my anorexia nervosa, my disease which I have come to accept as a long-term, lifetime part of me. Over time, that acceptance has been a shield. Emily still has some wins under her belt. Those things that matter in my recovery are positive self-talk, a psychiatrist and a dietician, which give me power to talk back and challenge her to FUCK OFF.

Do not let yourself, your emotions, become entangled with lurching waves of life that will in time without awareness, get you stuck. This process takes time, so be patient with yourself. Speak up for yourself. There are lots of little moments where people will come into your life like they did with mine, where you will find the impetus and reason to keep going.

I kept going one foot in front of the other; chipping away, little bit by little bit. Finding the right people to be in my inner circle meant finding people who would love me at my worst.

As I look back, I can still have my moments, but I know that my inner circle loves me and cheers me on to be successful every day even when I am not 100%. Having the right people, including health care professionals, in your corner is so important on this journey and I am forever grateful for how people gathered providing support on my journey. Remembering those parts of you, that you enjoy, and seeking those activities out matter in regaining your footing in yourself.

I am a survivor and thriver because I decided it was time to speak up and find help, love and hope that would dissolve and put an end to the poison from the secret that was slowly killing me from the inside out.

RHIANNON PARKER

Physical Education Teacher / Motivational Speaker
Connect: @rhiannonkateparker

LEIGH-ANNE HROMCIK
THE RISE & FALL FROM RESENTMENT TO REDEMPTION

E very time. Literally every time I finally surrendered, I would fall. I was falling faster every single time straight down to the never-ending darkness that was getting deeper with nowhere to land and no-one to catch me. My heart was pounding out of my chest, I was sweating and gasping for air. There was nothing for me to grab or hang onto, but it was up to me to save my own life. I screamed with every ounce of strength I had.

… With no-one to listen.

Just like all the other times, I was jolted awake and couldn't decipher what was real and what wasn't. Still trying to catch my breath, and looking around my bedroom, I was trying to make sense of my surroundings in hopes that I had just been stuck in another nightmare.

I lived in a state of severe sleep deprivation.

I was shaking my head back and forth as fast as I could to clear the heavy fog suffocating my thoughts. It seemed so hard to think straight, but strangely I was completely aware that I was struggling to navigate through the myriad of thoughts. Thoughts consisting of terror and impending doom. As my head began to clear, I realised it was just another nightmare.

Just like every other night I fell asleep.

Just another nightmare.

That's all.

Until I remembered I was *living* in a nightmare that would last for 315,532,807 seconds.

Give or take a few.

I was a single mom with two little ones when the living nightmare began. They were my world, and I felt an overwhelming sense of duty to safeguard my kids that went beyond my innate parental instincts due to the sensitive nature of the divorce from their father. My parents both passed away one year after my divorce was final. The circumstances of my divorce followed by the loss of my parents was terribly raw and painful.

My 'babies' were my family and I cherished them as if they were all I had in the world, holding them tightly to my heart.

Until my heart was shattered, and my life would never, ever be the same. Until death did I part from this earth.

Never underestimate the power of another human being's motives in life.

I don't know if the pain of losing those we love ever really goes away, but I was a master at wearing the 'I'm FINE' mask twenty-four seven.

FINE stands for fucked up, insecure, neurotic and emotional. So, there you have it. The FINE acronym may be a little strong, but as my story continued to unfold, I grew to check all four boxes of FINE as I found myself existing in a life of destruction, devastation, defeated, alone with no will to get back up.

I felt weak, destroyed and fear took up rent throughout my entire body. I found myself in disbelief asking, *How the HELL did I get here?* as I sat in the back seat with handcuffs on and the child safety doors locked so no-one could escape the back of the police car. I had never been in trouble in my entire life. The dispatcher was firing off codes on the radio one after the other, while I was trying to wrap my brain around how, why, who and what the hell just happened.

I was in my kitchen on a Sunday afternoon around 5:40pm staring at the worn-out recipe card that was stained from years of *her* cooking. I laid all the ingredients out (so I thought) to make Mom's infamous mouthwatering brisket and started reminiscing about what life was like before she was diagnosed with stage four cancer. I was lost in my thoughts as memories from my teenage years came rushing back to me. Painful memories.

I'm the youngest of two. My brother is three and a half years older than me and we grew up in a traditional family home with Dad being the breadwinner. Mom stayed home with us and took care of everything imaginable that comes with two kids in school and running a household.

I'm of the belief that our childhood experiences and upbringing create the foundation on which the rest of our lives are built. I also believe and experienced for myself that we can heal and change the trajectory of our lives and break generational cycles.

The memories came rushing back with such detail it felt as if I was experiencing the moments all over again. The most painful moments of my entire upbringing. Every single evening. Like clockwork.

She was in the kitchen, preparing to cook dinner as she grabbed the familiar glass, filled it with ice followed by vodka and grapefruit juice. I could literally hear the *clank, clank, clank* from the ice hitting the glass.

I knew the routine like clockwork. I also knew that I was safe for a couple of hours … Until … dinner was over. Mom made it clear she didn't need help cleaning up and insisted on doing the dishes alone.

Every dish, every night.

I would offer to help her every chance I could in hopes to make her 'happy'. I thought by helping her I would alleviate some of her chores and maybe, just maybe, that would keep her from turning into the woman I feared each night.

Like the night before.

… and the night before that.

… and the night before that.

… and so on.

I loved my mom dearly and always will even though she's left this earth, but the person she became as the evening progressed left deep scars on my heart and taught me that I wasn't worthy of love, or anything for that matter, unless the number on the scale told me I was.

As soon as she was done in the kitchen, I'd race to my bed and feign sleep to avoid being fed the laxatives she insisted I take. I couldn't make sense as to why her personality changed at night, but if I saw her eyes, abuse was on the horizon; normally a warm brown tint morphed into a cold darkness.

Was my mom mentally ill? I couldn't ask my dad. I tried that once. Only once because he shut me down and said I was ridiculous.

I was peeking through the door so I could see into the kitchen. I was literally spying on my own mom hoping to put the pieces of the puzzle together. I thought if I understood the why or what makes her change, maybe there's a way I could stop it?

No. I didn't have the power to stop it.

I watched her sip on the Almaden Rhine wine out of a wine glass that she hid in a small corner cabinet while she was doing the dishes.

Every night.

The same glass.

The same corner cabinet.

The same dark eyes.

She criticised my weight, shamed my body and called me names that I accepted as truth.

'Chubby.'

'Fat.'

'Double chin.

… and so on.

Sometimes she looked at me with disappointment and disgust, but the next day life appeared normal, but there was palpable tension that was 'our secret'. Looking back, that's the moment my relationship with *shame* was born.

I was in high school which came with all kinds of natural insecurities, wanting to be popular and fit in, yet stand out just enough to be seen but not feel uncomfortable.

Snapping back to reality, I was missing the key ingredient for the brisket so off to the store I went. A one-minute trip.

Purse in hand, I stepped out of my car and was face to face with a police officer. He seemed to appear out of nowhere.

He said, 'We received an anonymous call with your license plate and vehicle description allegedly driving recklessly. Have you had any alcohol to drink today?'

I'm thinking, *WTH?*

I replied truthfully. I mean, why wouldn't I? 'I had less than a glass of wine while I was cooking?' My intuition was screaming – something was off.

As time went on, I found out what really happened that day.

I was in shock and had no idea what was about to happen. The handcuffs were so tight, my wrists started bleeding onto his back seat. He smirked when he saw the blood.

There I was with my blonde hair, smeared make-up and thrown into a 'holding tank' with dozens of other women. From all walks of life. They just kept coming. It was a concrete dungeon from hell. The floors had accumulated decades of nastiness – I'll refrain from sharing. Two steel commodes lined the wall with no toilet paper in sight, other than the rolls people took to use as pillows. The conditions were deplorable – no soap, no towels, no privacy. Discoloured water was free if you were brave enough to drink straight from the nasty faucet. Once a day, bologna sandwiches were tossed into the tank onto the nasty floor. Woman would clamour over each other and fights erupted over the jail house delicacy. I learned things in that tank they don't teach in school. I wouldn't say it was useful information, but the master's degree in street smarts I obtained was priceless.

I felt a level of unrecognisable fear.

Terror.

I felt trapped.

I was trapped, traumatised and devastated.

Violence was at every turn in that holding tank.

Fifty-seven hours later, the guard yelled 'ATW!!!!' followed by my last name. ATW stands for 'all the way'. That was my cue that I was being released. I couldn't get out of there any faster. It was 3:12am and I was released to the streets without a ride, no money and a dead cell phone. I was standing outside the jail in the streets of downtown feeling defeated. I could smell the jail on my clothes, in my hair and everywhere around me. I remember the strong smell of urine coming from the streets, the humid sticky air and I could see random figures lurking in the darkness. The voices. They were the most terrifying of all because they came from every direction bouncing off the old, dirty brick walls that once supported a lively restaurant.

In that moment, I felt gratitude. Gratitude for the humid outdoor air despite the smell of urine. I could see the full moon that lit up the sky which reminded me that I was free.

For now.

Then the gut-wrenching news. I was speechless and ANGRY! Not just upset, but FURIOUS.

While I was 'away', my ex-husband had taken our kids out of the school system and moved them four hours away to live with his sister. Already enrolled in a new school where they didn't know anyone, let alone did they anticipate their lives were about to be turned upside-down and they'd be ripped away from their mother.

That was the first time I felt as if my spirit and soul didn't just die, but they had been murdered.

I stood in my kitchen again; looking at the spoiled brisket that sat on the island next to the marinade. There on the island sat the quarter-full glass of wine that reminded me of my mom before, but now it took on an entirely new meaning.

I was alone. Very alone. I had no idea what to do next or who to call, but I knew my kids needed to hear from Mommy. They were scared, confused and scarred.

That. Did. Not. Have. To. Happen.

They were innocent, they didn't ask for this and most definitely didn't deserve it.

I felt this overwhelming sense of desperation to connect with their little hearts. It surpassed the innate need a mother is gifted with to nurture and protect. As I was still standing in the kitchen my entire body from my scalp to the end of my toes started to shake uncontrollably. I couldn't stop the shaking and right before the room started spinning, the spasms took on a life of their own. The room picked up speed and spun me around in circles faster and faster until it stopped.

I lost consciousness and collapsed, but before I hit the tile floor, I slammed my head on the kitchen island countertop and landed in a pile of fresh blood from the cut on my head.

Unconscious.

Alone.

Barely hanging on to life.

I wrestled with anger, fear, desperation and inconsolable separation anxiety from my kids that left an enormous gaping hole in my heart, soul and spirit. I went from being the mom that was involved in all of my kids' school and extracurricular activities to a lonely existence which was exacerbated when isolation set in. I resigned from my volunteer commitment at church and sat alone in church. Until I stopped going altogether.

When I made it to the grocery store, I couldn't even make eye contact with the cashier.

When I bumped into an acquaintance at the store, I was met with eyes filled with judgement.

The *shame* intensified.

I wanted to scream at the top of my lungs, 'That's not who I am! You don't understand! There was a motive!'

An unconceivable motive to hide the dark secret underneath my new image as an unfit mother.

As I stood there in front of the judge, it was time for me to speak. The *only* time I was allowed to speak.

Guilty.

Not guilty.

No contest.

I could feel every muscle in my body tighten up as I tried not to lose my balance. My conservative navy suit with modest heels became my official 'court outfit' for years to come —although I had no idea what my future would hold as I stood there on that terrifying day of judgement.

Conviction day. The day that served as the catalyst to my never-ending *shame and blame cycle.*

As the world went on living around me, I lived only to fight for my kids.

I began to notice my patterns. I was either a rule follower to the extreme or I had rebellious tendencies, but I was never a malicious, violent or selfish human being that intentionally caused harm to others.

That wasn't and isn't in my DNA, but on paper my life began to look as if I was every one of those things and worse as my permanent file within 'the system' grew at every turn in my life.

I completed my probation terms successfully and was granted 'joint custody' on one condition. I could see my kids for six hours every other Saturday if I hired a home health aide to supervise every minute of our precious time.

Shame. Blame. Resentment.

Resentment is said to be like drinking poison with the expectation that the other person will suffer. I held onto resentment for years which felt like a slow miserable attempt at suicide.

The toxic cycle of shame and blame took control of my life. I didn't have a clue it was happening back then. I knew the difference between right and wrong intellectually, but there was an indescribable level of emotional pain that was at war with my rational mind. The pain felt unbearable. I couldn't breathe. I was hopeless and I just wanted it to stop.

I barely remember buying the wine. Not because I was intoxicated, but as if I was checked out of my own life as a coping mechanism or maybe it was the hopeless state of mind I existed in.

The exact thing that landed me in jail the first time was the exact thing that landed me in jail the second time.

… the third time was the worst.

The insanity of it all was that I began to self-sabotage my own life that I had worked so hard to rebuild. I carried the compounded shame from before and every time I closed my eyes, I saw the eyes of judgement, heard the detention officers screaming at me, the judge looking down at me with disgust and the absolute worst of all of it was the thought of letting my kids down after all of this time. They began to trust me again and our relationships continued to grow stronger, but as long as I still carried the heavy burden of shame from my past, I would be a *prisoner of shame.*

My own shame.

Even though I was sober for years at a time, I was still 'sick' inside because of the toxic emotions that continued to fester day after day.

The attempt to numb my pain with alcohol was short-lived (as opposed to months or years) and never ended well. I stopped eating altogether because my body began rejecting anything I put in it. Including the alcohol that was meant to kill my pain. I did what the insanity told me to do.

I forced myself to consume more alcohol hoping something would anesthetise the gaping hole where my emotional pain lived.

It didn't work.

Ever.

It only created more sickness in both my mind and body.

I've only shared this with one person prior to this book, but during those years, there was a defining moment that I allowed to hold me hostage for years. During one of the family court proceedings, I overheard a conversation. 'I wish she would just die because [she] is a better mother to the kids.'

That was it. I was off to the races desperately trying to escape from the snippet I had just overheard.

To no avail.

That would once again result in another visit to jail. Handcuffs, police car. Navy suit, modest heels, same judge, and this time she came down on me with a vengeance.

I had two choices. Twelve months in county jail or an inpatient treatment centre for no less than forty-five days followed by two years of probation depending on my treatment progress. If there was any hope that I could remove the *shackles of shame*, I was willing to give it a try.

26 August is the anniversary of my mom's death. It also happens to be the anniversary of the incident when I inexplicitly felt my body rolling several times across the freeway in rush hour traffic until I landed on my back. The pavement had destroyed the parts of my body that weren't covered by my sundress leaving severe skin injuries, some as deep as the bone. I just laid there looking up at the blue sky and white fluffy clouds then said, 'I'm coming to see you, Mom.' The last thing I remember was looking at my feet. Despite the tragic accident that had just happened, my flip flops which had the word *Faith* embroidered on them hadn't moved in the slightest bit. It was and always has been God that protected me. I was rushed to a nearby hospital before being transferred to a psychiatric hospital for five days of observation to make sure I wasn't

suicidal. I wasn't suicidal, but I had lost the will to live.

With two black eyes, a fractured tailbone, broken right scapula and severe skin injuries from that hot pavement, I arrived at the treatment centre seven hours away from home. I spent ninety days there surrounded by other women with their own set of challenges. For the first time in my life, I finally felt understood. They got me and I got them. Judgement didn't exist between all of us, and I experienced the beauty of unconditional love and support by people who lifted me up instead of tearing me down. That ninety-day experience showed me I was capable of connecting to another human being at a level and depth that I didn't know I craved. As far back as my high school years, I dealt with feelings of abandonment and loneliness. I felt none of that here. We were similar, had our own unique differences just as God created us to be, but we were on the same path in life and these ladies became my sisters. I found an insurmountable amount of peace with my new family. A peace that was foreign to me, but it felt like I was home. Finally.

Two and half more years went by, but this time I was in 'sober court' which was probation on steroids. I was full of gratitude as graduation from the program approached. I was asked to speak at graduation which was a huge honour. I stood next to the judge and smiled for the photo just before I walked onto the stage to speak. The audience was packed with family, including little ones running around with such innocence. It was a beautiful sight, but inside there was a lingering pain that felt like a knife went through my heart. No-one was there for me.

Fast-forward a few years later, I had started a couple of businesses, bought a new home, was up by 4am to spend a few quiet moments with God and hit the gym/crossfit by 5am.

… But then.

I accepted an invite to lunch with the coach, but I had no idea how uncomfortable I felt in my own skin until we sat face to face. I had a past and he had no idea.

… Fear of abandonment settled in.

We grew closer, and my inner critic grew louder.

So did the voice of insanity, *Take a few sips to relax your nerves.*

The insanity of doing the same thing over and over expecting different results.

Then it happened. Strike three – automatic felony.

The 'why' I listened didn't matter; *it mattered that I listened.*

… The ending never changed.

I had a felony.

I was a felon.

I am a felon.

I received a life sentence that day branded with the scarlet letter 'F'. A felony DWI that can never be sealed or expunged.

… Until death do I part from it.

Same navy suit, modest heels, felony court this time. I never saw the judge up close, but I felt the punishment every day of my life going forward:

Five years of probation, ten years in prison if I failed probation at any time, for any reason.

Two pages of conditions, restrictions and rules.

$10,000 fine, not including thousands of other charges.

Random drug and alcohol testing.

Hair follicle testing.

Home breathalyser requiring mandatory testing three times a day (5,475 plus blows into this device).

… And so on.

I threw the navy suit and modest heels in the trash and felt the chains loosen.

I was grateful for five years of probation, that I never caused an accident, hurt anyone (other than myself and those that cared about me) or even got pulled over for a DWI; which is backwards, I know. That's another story for another time.

I never went to prison.

I completed the five years successfully, carried PTSD with me. During those five years, anxiety hit an all-time high. Not because I was violating my probation, but because life isn't fair. The system isn't always fair, and I witnessed injustice and abuse firsthand.

Once you're in the system, you're in the system unless you isolate from society.

A few years ago, I met the woman in the mirror and believe she's exactly who God created me to be. I learned to love my imperfections. Stopped self-sabotaging my life. The generational cycle of alcohol abuse was broken! My children went through their own hell and have the scars to prove it. I earned their trust again and today my beautiful twenty-one-year-old daughter and I are closer than I could have dreamt of. The relationship with my twenty-four-year-old son is improving. He's grown into a young man and I've met the woman in the mirror so I pray we'll continue to get to know the mother and son we are today. God willing.

Shame loves silence and blame cannot live without his twin sister, shame.

Abusing alcohol or getting a DWI (or more) doesn't mean someone is an 'alcoholic'. That's a controversial statement that I'd never make if I couldn't back it up with evidence. If someone is an alcoholic, that doesn't mean they're homeless, dishonest and drinking out of a brown paper sack.

Some are, most are not.

After the felony, I was hell-bent on uncovering what I was trying to escape all along.

I removed every distraction, cell phone included and created a safe place and space. If I needed to scream, cry or dance, I needed any resistance removed. I kept this sacred process to myself and protected my space and place as if my life depended on it. Which it did. The general idea was to allow myself to just 'be'. Whatever that looked like in the moment. I followed a series of prompts that acted as the catalyst to peeling back the layers of my life. I gave myself permission to freely experience each layer no matter how messy it was. The messier the better. The more rigorously honest, the more transformational. The DEEPEST transformational method was born and trademarked from that very day where I turned myself inside-out, faced the good, the bad and the ugly head-on.

Messy is a daily goal for me now.

I removed the 'I'm FINE' mask because at some point, your truth will be revealed.

As a felon, I was unemployable, other than a few select companies open to hiring felons. If I wanted to pursue a career where I could tap into my purpose and make an impact while I'm still here on this earth, then it was up to me to make it happen.

I've started five companies with several more I'd like to acquire.

I'm ineligible to rent a house or apartment, so I immersed myself in the steps I needed to take in order to qualify for a mortgage loan on my own. *I did whatever it took to make it happen.*

I moved in two years ago.

I'm not special in that regard; I believe the one thing that differentiates me from someone who's still stuck in the BS is:

I mastered the ability to leverage my rebellious side to use as fuel to do WHATEVER IT TAKES, NO MATTER WHAT in the face of adversity, obstacles, rejections. It's non-negotiable and will be until ...

My mission in life is to be intentional every single day about how I show up in this world which starts with the commitment to show up for myself first. My intention is to stay open, vulnerable, uncomfortable and share my truth to create a safe space for someone else to do the same.

'Don't let your past
Blackmail your present
To ruin your future.' Leigh Anne H.

LEIGH-ANNE HROMCIK

The Author of Redemption

Connect: unleashandrelease.com / @leighanne_hromcik

PSALM WOOCHING
A FRAGILE DREAM

always heard people say that God breaks you down to build you up, and even though it sounds so cliché, it played out right in front of my own eyes, for me and my life.

You see, I asked God why he chose to give me ability, why he chose to put me in these places I was fortunate enough to be in as a rugby union player, in front of thousands of people. Why he chose to make me into this person he had, only to tear me down and take it all away from me when I was at the pinnacle of my life, both personally and professionally.

Growing up, I was an average kid. I had no real big dreams, as such. I never considered myself special or exceptional in any way. I wasn't strong, nor was I confident. I didn't have a path, per say, I didn't know what I wanted from life yet.

I was fortunate to have grown up in Hawaii, in the islands. It was a place where the sun kissed the earth, where the waves crashed against the shore in a rhythmic melody and where the vibrant colours of nature painted a breathtaking canvas. It was a place where time seemed to slow down, where worries dissolved in the ocean breeze and where the spirit of aloha permeated every aspect of life.

Life in Hawaii was simple and humble. My parents, my pillars of strength, instilled in me a deep appreciation for the land, the gifts it provided and a profound sense of cultural pride and belonging. Their love and sacrifices shaped the person I was and still am to this day. The values they not only instilled in me but the importance of family, community and tradition – values deeply rooted in our Samoan culture.

We lived off the land, nurturing it as it nurtured us. My days were filled with exploration, venturing out into the islands, diving into crystal-clear waters and climbing the mountains that framed our island paradise.

In this idyllic atmosphere, I found solace and a sense of belonging. The worries of the world melted away as I immersed myself in the beauty that surrounded me. Nature became my playground, and with each adventure, I discovered something new about myself and the world around me.

Freshman year of high school – a time of transition, new beginnings and the pressure to fit in. For most kids, it meant joining a sports team, immersing themselves in the world of competition and camaraderie. But for me, sports didn't resonate the same way. I played football, and to put it bluntly, I was terrible. I was merely a body added to the roster, lacking the natural skill and passion that my peers seemed to possess effortlessly.

Rugby, on the other hand, was in my blood. With my father being Samoan, the sport was deeply ingrained in my heritage. But as strange as it may sound, it didn't ignite that same fire within me. Sports, in general, failed to connect me to my true self. Instead, it was the land, the ocean – the elements of nature – that made me feel at home.

As I entered high school, the pressure to conform intensified, especially from friends who were deeply involved in sports. I felt a sense of obligation, a need to fit in, to appease the expectations of others. But deep down, I knew that my heart wasn't in it. The added pressure from my parents, who always lovingly pushed me to participate, only fuelled my resentment towards sports.

That first year of high school was a struggle. From all angles, I felt the weight of peer pressure bearing down on me. The desire to belong clashed with my inner voice, telling me that there must be more to life than conforming to societal norms. It was a time of confusion, of searching for my true identity and purpose.

But as the saying goes, God works in mysterious ways.

Just as I was navigating this internal struggle, the summer rolled around and I found myself in Washington, visiting my grandparents. My grandfather, knowing my love for the outdoors, took me to a university to give me a glimpse of what that life could look like for me.

As we approached the university, my eyes widened in amazement. The football stadium stood before me, grand and imposing. The energy in the air was palpable, and I couldn't help but be captivated by the sense of community and passion that surrounded the world of college athletics. It was in that moment, as I stood in awe, that my grandfather uttered words that would forever change the trajectory of my life.

'You can go to these schools by playing sports, Psalm,' he said, his voice filled with a mix of wisdom and encouragement.

Like a bolt of lightning coursing through my entire body, something clicked within me. It was as if the universe had conspired to open my eyes to the possibilities that lay before me. In that instant, my goals became clear, my purpose crystallised. At fifteen years old, I made a declaration to myself, a commitment that would shape the years to come.

'I'm going to play in one of these big schools,' I proclaimed with unwavering determination.

From that moment, everything changed. The switch flipped within me, and my perspective on sports shifted entirely. It was no longer about fitting in or appeasing others. It became about being the best version of myself on the field and in the classroom, with the singular aim of reaching that lofty goal I had set for myself.

I poured my heart and soul into my studies and my athletic pursuits. I no longer saw them as separate entities but as interconnected pieces of a puzzle, both contributing to my journey towards that coveted opportunity to play at a prestigious university. Each day became an opportunity to push myself harder, to hone my skills and to prove to myself that I was capable of achieving greatness.

But it wasn't just about sports anymore. Education became my ally, my gateway to a brighter future. A total 180 came in to play for me, I changed schools; I realised that success on the field could only be sustained if I also excelled academically. I had to get not only my physicality in the game but my mind. So, I became a dedicated student, driven by the belief that education would serve as the foundation for those dreams to become a reality for me.

Throughout high school, I continued to persevere, even when faced with setbacks and doubts. The road was far from easy, and there were moments when I questioned my own abilities. But that initial revelation, that glimpse into a world of possibilities, remained etched in my mind, a constant reminder of the path I had chosen for myself and it gave me a burning fire inside, something I had never felt before, I knew this was me, my forever, my purpose if you will, even at fifteen. I went up to the school with this confidence and told them in which position I was going to play. There was just an innate feeling with guidance happening in my life that gave me sheer confidence in what I was doing and speaking it into my reality.

And so, as I moved through high school, each step brought me closer to my goal. The school gave me that chance to prove myself – and I did. I put a lot of work in on the off-season, and it was hard, but the challenges and sacrifices became my stepping stones, moulding me into a stronger, more resilient version of myself. It was a time of self-discovery, of embracing my individuality and of realising that my worth was not determined by others' opinions but by my own belief in what I could achieve and I set out to prove it. My day's schedule was simply to be training to become the best.

I put the hard yards in both academically and on the field, day in and day out, and I began to reap the benefits, my talent started to shine.

By the time I was going into my third year, those goals I had set in my mind were slowly turning into reality as I climbed the ranks, gaining the title of best player in the islands, then in the country.

Senior year rolled around, and as the final season of high school approached, I felt the weight of anticipation and uncertainty. The calls from big schools hadn't come in yet, and the noise around me grew louder – people telling me that I couldn't make it, that I was too small, that I wasn't good enough. But instead of allowing those words to break me, they fuelled the fire within me.

With determination, I entered my senior season with a burning desire to prove all the doubters wrong. I poured my heart and soul into every practice, every game, pushing myself beyond my limits. And then, like a dream becoming a reality, the calls started coming in – from big schools, the ones that people said were out of my reach.

It was a testament to the power of hard work, perseverance and sacrifice. All the doubts and criticisms I faced only fuelled my determination to succeed. And when I finally received offers from prestigious universities, it was an overwhelming feeling of triumph and validation. One by one, I listened to those who had doubted me, silenced by the undeniable proof that I was good enough, that I had earned my place among the best.

Signing with the University of Washington was the culmination of all my dreams. The emotions were indescribable – elation, relief and a deep sense of accomplishment. It was a validation of all the years of hard work, dedication and unwavering belief in myself. I had made it. I had reached the goal I had set for myself, and it was an affirmation that I was on the right path.

But as quickly as the elation washed over me, I was brought back down to earth in a humbling way. Stepping onto campus, I was once again the new guy, starting from square one. The fire that had fuelled my journey burned within me, reminding me that I had done it once, and I could do it all over again.

I became a go-getter, unyielding in my pursuit of greatness. Nobody was going to tell me what I could or couldn't achieve. I felt a deep sense of mental strength, an unbreakable spirit that permeated every aspect of my life. I was ready to lift the world on my back if I had to, to conquer any challenge that lay before me.

As my story continued to unfold, I found myself climbing the rankings year after year. In my first year, I played a small role, but with each passing season, I earned more playing time, excelling on the field. Through the constant grind, the countless hours of hard work, I witnessed my growth and development. In my last three years, I achieved remarkable success, climbing the ranks and making a name for myself.

And then, in my very last year, I reached the pinnacle. I earned the role of 'the man' on defence, becoming a stand-out player in the eyes of my teammates, coaches and fans. The goals, the visions that were placed on my heart at fifteen years old, were playing out before my eyes. I was living it. The games, the newspaper articles, the interviews – I became the centre of attention, the voice of the university.

But it wasn't just about athletic success. Academically, I excelled too. I found myself on the dean's list, pursuing a degree in medical anthropology. I balanced my passion for sports with a commitment to education, knowing that true success encompassed both aspects of my life.

From the outside looking in, it appeared that I had the perfect life. I was predicted to go to the NFL, earning fame and fortune. I had everything – a promising career, a loving girlfriend who was a professional softball player and a bright future. My heart, with the belief that I had the means to take care of my family, to give back to my parents who had sacrificed so much for me.

Then the proposal came next to my girlfriend, it was featured on ESPN, Fox News and other major channels. Quite literally, my life was playing out in the public eye. It seemed as if my whole life had been set up perfectly.

In the aspect of my career in football, the achievements were there, and I had all I thought I ever wanted.

But there suddenly became a deep sense of something missing within my soul which began playing out over and over. I felt a yearning, a desire to pursue another sport – one that connected me to my heritage and fulfilled my father's dreams.

Rugby, the sport that ran through my blood, called out to me. Again, that feeling of 'knowing' came to me just as it had at fifteen years of age 'knowing what I wanted to exactly do with my life'. It was time to step away from the path I had carved for myself in American football and explore new horizons.

The pinnacle of one dream marked the beginning of another. And with the same fire and determination that had fuelled me thus far, I embarked on a new chapter, following in the footsteps of my father and embracing the rich heritage that shaped me.

As I took off my helmet for the last time, the weight of finality settled upon my shoulders. It was the end of my football journey, but deep within, I knew that the calling to rugby was too strong to ignore. The sport that ran through my veins beckoned me, and I made the bold decision to pursue it wholeheartedly. I announced my transition on social media, and the response was overwhelming – waves of support and encouragement flooded in.

Within months, a remarkable turn of events unfolded. I was chosen to play for the USA International Rugby team. The magnitude of this opportunity was not lost on me. It was unheard of to go from not playing rugby for five or six years to receiving a call-up to represent the international team. Moreover, I was informed that I would be playing a completely new position. The challenges ahead seemed daunting, but deep down, I knew that this was the path I was meant to take.

The influx of support and belief from the rugby community fuelled my determination to prove myself. It was as if the universe once more had conspired to give me this chance, to show that God doesn't always call the qualified but instead qualifies the called. The scripture resonated deeply with me, affirming that I had been chosen for a purpose beyond my comprehension.

Stepping onto the international stage, I carried with me the weight of the expectations placed upon me. It was a risk for any international team to invest in someone who had been away from the game for so long and was transitioning into a new position. But that didn't deter me. I embraced the challenge with unwavering commitment, knowing that this was the opportunity of a lifetime.

As I moved forward in my rugby journey, the path seemed to unfold before me. Within months, contracts started pouring in from top-tier clubs in Italy, France and England. I was travelling the world, loving every moment. The highs I had experienced in football were now reaching their zenith in rugby.

And not only was I pursuing my dreams, but my fiancée was also at the top of her sporting profession, representing the USA in her respective sport. Our journeys were intertwined, our passion for sports fuelling our shared pursuit of greatness. It was a remarkable synchronicity, a testament to the power of dreams and the support we found in each other.

As I soared to new heights in rugby, I experienced the joy of competing at the pinnacle of the sport. The crowds cheered my name, the accolades piled up and my impact on the field was undeniable. I embraced the challenges of my new position, honing my skills and pushing myself beyond my limits.

I believed that God had chosen me for something great, that I was destined for success. I was proud of my accomplishments. I was blessed with natural talent, with opportunities that others never had. I was grateful, always on camera, acknowledging that my successes were gifts from a higher power to everyone. Always pointing to the sky and thanking my accomplishments to God in front of the crowds.

But life has a way of testing all of us, and my turn was about to hit me.

Just as I reached the apex of my everything, life struck me one of my biggest blows that shook my world and turned it completely upside down and this is where my story takes a turn …

In an instant, my world came crashing down, as if a tidal wave of despair had swept me away.

A single phone call that would be the start of shattering my dreams and leaving me broken in every sense of the word.

Physically, experiencing a pain that would reverberate through my entire body. Emotionally, a raw ache that would be insurmountable. And spiritually, questioning the very essence of my being.

The Psalm who had once stood tall, who exuded strength and confidence, would suddenly become a fragile little boy lost in the depths of despair. The weight that I had once boasted of carrying with ease would become an unbearable burden, threatening to crush me beneath its weight.

I remember that day with vivid clarity. The call came from my fiancée at the time, the words, 'We need to talk when you get back from Vancouver, enjoy,' hung in the air. Deep within me, an intuitive sense told me that something devastating awaited me on the other end of that conversation.

As the minutes ticked by, each second seemed to stretch into eternity. Fear gripped me as thoughts raced through my mind, images of shattered dreams and irreparable loss flashing in my mind, even though the conversation hadn't even taken place yet.

I had been called in the middle of the season, and hearing those words, having that intuitive sense something devastating was awaiting me and those thoughts racing through my mind, I knew I had to leave right then and there. So I did, I simply grabbed my things, told my childhood friends whom I had brought to Vancouver with me, 'If you don't see me Monday, it means I took a plane back home to Hawaii and I will be there,' got in the car and set off to a conversation I didn't know if I was ready for.

I braced myself for the storm, knowing that whatever lay ahead could and would ultimately change the course of my life forever, and whatever lay ahead I knew that if something bad was about to happen, I was leaving for home – my home, the islands, Hawaii.

That conversation finally happened, the moment of truth, the reality before me.

As the words spilled out of my fiancée's mouth, those feelings I had racing through my mind when I first heard 'we need to talk' confirmed all I had thought.

I felt the ground beneath me give way. It was a gut-wrenching revelation, a blow that struck at the very core of my being. The dreams we had built, the future I had envisioned for us, crumbled around me. The weight of the news pressed upon me, threatening to drown me in a sea of despair. The wedding – our wedding was in a month's time. Thoughts racing through my mind, what had changed? This was the woman I loved, the woman I would lay down my life for.

In that moment, I felt the fragility of life, the unpredictable nature of our existence. Just as I had felt God had conspired me through my successes, here I was feeling as if God had conspired to strip away the illusions of invincibility and remind me of my vulnerability. The strong facade I had crafted over the years shattered, revealing the raw vulnerability beneath.

But why me? Why now? What had I done to deserve such a cruel turn of events? Why had God decided to strip away my everything?

As the day led into night, the weight of my emotions became unbearable. Every fibre of my being ached, and I could feel the exhaustion take over my body. It was a draining experience, not just for me but for both of us.

The shattered dreams had left us wounded, searching for solace in a world that suddenly seemed unfamiliar.

With a heavy heart, I gathered my belongings and tossed them into a duffle bag. Without a second thought, I climbed into an Uber with a one-way destination to the airport in mind, booking my ticket on my phone as I went, desperately seeking an escape from the pain I was experiencing.

Home beckoned me, not just any home, but the embrace of the islands – the place where my spirit found solace, where I thought the healing balm of nature could hopefully help what I was feeling and mend my now broken soul.

The road stretched out before me, winding and twisting like the path of my own journey. Each mile marker passed by in a blur, catching the flight, I watched the scenery changing from above seeing the bustling city streets below to finally, the serene beauty of the islands coming into view yet all vaguely clear to me, as my eyes were constantly glazed with fighting back my tears.

As I arrived, the island, my home, embraced me with open arms, as if it had been waiting for my return. The whispers of the ocean waves soothed my restless heart for moments. The palm trees swayed in the breeze, their leaves moving in harmony with the ebb and flow of my emotions.

I walked along the familiar shores, feeling the sand beneath my feet, grounding me in the present moment. But still, even in that moment, I felt like I was losing Psalm, I was losing me to the pain I was experiencing.

I retreated into myself, enveloped by a cloud of confusion and grief. The confident Psalm, the one who had believed he could conquer any challenge, faltered under the weight of this devastating blow. I questioned everything – my worth, my purpose, my identity. It felt as though not just a piece of me, but all of me had been ripped away, leaving an empty void that seemed impossible to fill.

The feelings of sadness that had gripped me were only the beginning of a downward spiral that seemed to have no end. As I thought I had moved past the sadness, a barrage of other unsettling experiences washed over me, dragging me further into the depths of despair. I found myself in a state of constant turmoil – mentally detached, devoid of happiness, my vision blurred, plagued by sleepless nights haunted by unsettling visions. My heart raced with palpitations, twitches in my legs, I was seeking answers to the torment that consumed me.

Month after month, I sought solace in medical specialists, traversing the islands in search of an explanation for my pain. Brain scans, consultations with experts and countless tests were conducted, only to reveal that physically, I was fine. Yet, deep within, I knew that my struggles were rooted in something more profound – my mental wellbeing. The truth stared back at me like a mirror, demanding to be acknowledged.

While the old version of Psalm attempted to justify the pain, grasping at the possibility of brain damage from my athletic career, the truth loomed larger. I sought more tests, more opinions, hoping to find evidence that would validate my suffering. But time and again, the results came back normal, leaving me with the unsettling realisation that my battle was within.

Months turned into an agonising blur as I continued to deteriorate. Emotions swallowed me whole, consuming every fibre of my being. The passion for life that once burned brightly within me had eroded, leaving a void that seemed impossible to fill.

Then, on a day that felt like a lifeline, an opportunity presented itself – Why Wam, a place that held deep significance in my life. It was more than just a Christian university; it was a part of my childhood, where my parents had met, where my father had served in the kitchens, feeding the souls of thousands. And here, in my darkest hour, stood a beacon of hope – an unexpected encounter with my heritage.

Why did the universe lead me to this place on that particular day?

As I sat in the cafe, engulfed in the depths of my despair, I grappled with the reality that the strong Psalm, the one I had once known, was fading away. The emotional Psalm I had become felt foreign, and I could no longer bear the weight of the disconnect. Desperate, I cried out to God, questioning why and how all of this was happening to me. In that moment of vulnerability, I pleaded for answers, seeking solace in the familiar surroundings of my childhood.

Then, like a thunderclap piercing through the darkness, clarity washed over me – the most vivid communication from God I had ever experienced. The question resonated within me: What was my testimony? What story did I want to tell? I had adorned myself with fame, accolades and symbols of faith, but was it all an act? Was my praise to God genuine, or was I merely playing a role, a puppeteer manipulating the image of a Christian athlete?

In that moment of revelation, I realised that my motives had been misplaced. I had been so focused on external validation and the image of success that I had lost sight of my authentic relationship with God. The encounter felt like a mirror held up before me, forcing me to confront my own truths – to acknowledge that I had been living a facade.

The weight of my question – 'Why did you take everything from me?' – led to a profound realisation. God's response echoed through my being, challenging me to examine my motives. Had I truly praised and thanked Him authentically for the height of fame I had reached? The truth struck me with a jolt of clarity – God had allowed me to be tested, to see if the real Psalm would continue to give glory, even when stripped of everything.

At that moment, my eyes were opened, and I confronted the realisation that I had been driven by the wrong reasons. My faith had become entangled with the pursuit of worldly success and public acclaim. The journey had become more about my image than about my relationship with God.

In that cafe, my heart humbled and vulnerable, I made a solemn pledge to redefine my faith, to reclaim my authenticity. It was a pivotal moment – a rebirth of purpose, a shedding of the layers that had obscured the true essence of who I was meant to be.

And in that place of confrontation – a sacred space where I was stripped of the persona I had become, taken back to the essence of the little boy who had once roamed these shores, I began volunteering at the very spot where I had encountered God. Tiger and Blake, two guys who ran the place, took me under their wings. I poured out my heart to them, confessing that I was an athlete who had been recognised throughout the islands, but here, in this sacred space, I wanted to be known simply as Psalm. I was ready to embrace humility, to clean the gym and to engage in tasks I had never before encountered.

For the next nine months, I immersed myself in the process of rebuilding. I allowed myself to be humbled, to strip away the layers of fame and success and to rediscover the true essence of who I was. Each day, as I breathed in the salty air, a sense of renewal washed over me, rekindling the fire within my soul.

The weight of shattered dreams began to lift, replaced by a new-found determination to rebuild and rise above disappointment. I found solace in the simplicity of island life – the unhurried pace, the authenticity of human connections and the ability to find joy in the smallest moments. As I reconnected with myself, the real Psalm emerged from the ashes.

In the embrace of the island, I rediscovered the passions that had once fuelled my spirit – the love for the land, the ocean and the thrill of adventure. It was here, amidst the waves and the gentle rustle of palm trees, that I unlocked the resilience that lay dormant within me.

The island was bringing me close to God who became my guiding light, reminding me that I was not defined by the shattered dreams, but by the strength that resided deep within my being. It was a reminder that

He, God, had brought me home to reveal the truth.

Days turned into weeks, and I surrendered myself to the healing powers of the island and to God. It was a process of rebirth, guided by faith and the unwavering belief that there was a purpose for all I had endured. I let go of my own desires, and I allowed God to guide me on this transformative path.

As I opened my heart to His guidance, I began to witness the beauty of His plan unfolding before me.

The island became my sanctuary – a space where I sought solace, where I reconnected with my roots and where I deepened my relationship with him. The healing was not just physical or emotional, but spiritual in its essence. It was a reawakening, a rekindling of the flame of faith that had flickered within me.

In this sacred space, I learned to surrender, to trust and to listen to the whispers of my heart. I connected back to my roots, to the rich history and enduring legacy. I found strength and resilience in hearing once more the stories of my ancestors who navigated the vast Pacific Ocean, preserving their culture and heritage through generations. Hearing about their indomitable spirit and ability to adapt to changing circumstances, my eyes were being opened.

God led me through the darkness, unveiling the purpose of my existence. It was not about accolades or fame – it was about embracing humility, compassion and the power of a genuine connection with others.

With each passing day, I witnessed the transformation within myself. The mask of the false Psalm, the one driven by external validation, had crumbled, revealing the authentic version of who I was meant to be.

I no longer sought the spotlight or the applause of the crowds; instead, I embraced the unseen moments, where God's love and grace could be shared in the simplest of acts.

As I walked this path, I learned to let go of the need for answers, to surrender to the unknown and to trust that every step was part of a greater plan. The journey was not without its challenges, its doubts and its moments of struggle, but through it all, my faith remained steadfast.

I clung to the belief that God had brought me to this island to show me the power of his love, the importance of humility and the true meaning of redemption.

In the sanctuary of the island and in the presence of God, I found my purpose. I discovered that my story was not about fame or material success, but about the transformation that could be sparked by embracing my authentic self and living a life of love, compassion and faith.

And in due time, in the stillness of the island, I found clarity. The chaos of the world faded into the background, and my focus shifted to the essence of what truly mattered – the relationships, the love, the pursuit of a purpose greater than myself.

The island became a sanctuary, a sanctuary where I could heal, reflect and gather the strength to rebuild.

As I prepared to leave the island and return to the outside world, I carried within me a renewed sense of purpose and a deep gratitude for the journey I had travelled and to fully give myself to God.

I knew God, through the island, had shown me the power of resilience, the beauty of surrender and the capacity of the human spirit to rise again, even when faced with shattered dreams.

With God as my guide, I set forth on a new path – one that would honour the lessons learned, the resilience discovered and the unwavering belief that no matter how dark the night may seem, the dawn will always break.

Now as I progress through life, I am continually reminded of the importance of cherishing my roots and preserving our cultural legacy. Every success I achieve is not just mine alone, but a collective celebration of my family and community, my ancestors' dreams and the hard work of those who came before me.

Being rooted in my Samoan heritage has given my life meaning, purpose and direction. It has shaped my values, perspectives and aspirations, grounding me in a world that can often feel chaotic and uncertain. I take great pride in being a torchbearer of my culture, sharing its richness with the world and striving to pass it on to the generations that will follow. My journey is not just my own; it's a continuation of the narrative that began long before I was born.

In moments of self-doubt or uncertainty, I draw strength from the knowledge that I am part of a resilient and vibrant lineage. My parents' teachings and my Samoan heritage serve as a constant reminder that I can overcome anything, embracing challenges with courage and perseverance.

And armed with the strength God refilled within me, I know that I have the power to rebuild at anytime, to forge a future filled with hope, purpose and a deep connection to Him, God, my roots and to me, Psalm Fa'afoisia Pulemagafa Wooching.

PSALM WOOOCHING

Pro Athlete Rugby Player
Connect: @psalmwooching

KAREN LEDBURY
COURAGE UNVEILED: A JOURNEY OF HEALING

I have discovered courage has been inside of me for most of my life untapped until recently. Being raised in rural Queensland gives you a fountain of opportunities to develop such character. Character that is universally found in every language across this great expanse of our world.

Courage means knowing how to respond to a difficulty without fear. The essence of courage comes from a clarity of mind, the test of your mettle, spirit, tenacity, mental or moral strength, firmness of mindset and will in the face of danger or hardship. Carrying courage in your life toolbox enables you to face with certainty those experiences that stretch your self-will like a rubber band.

To stretch like a rubber band, you need a pivot point. My pivoting point has been turning negatives into positives. Positive pivot points that arm you with an opportunity to find joy, delight, hope and gratitude with each choice. It is up to you to discover characteristics within to fuel positive pivot points when navigating through the wildness of life to create happiness and belonging when change is present.

We never know what will come our way in life, good or bad. With certainty we can count on life being full of changes. Courage and positivity helped me to look at all change as a precious gift and to find the ray of hope in each and every day to ensure we are present with gratitude for all we have and the challenges that face us.

I have faced many pivotal points in my life and none more so than the past two years. In 2021 where we were pandemic driven. Engulfed by harsh standards that limited living with freedoms that now we appreciate. We all know the feeling of that time, its debilitating constrictions for the greater good of the group and society. During that time, I needed to summon all of my patience and courage.

I had tried unsuccessfully several times to enter Queensland to visit my dad. He had been sick, but this was different, this was more serious. This was a dark cloud that had a time line. Upon seeing the words, 'You are accepted,' it was like all the time and effort needed just vanished and was replaced with my pocket full of sunshine, my hope, my heart filled with gratitude and my soul forever soothed knowing I would have one more precious moment with my beautiful dad, the man who shaped me.

As the plane touched down on the tarmac, of that sleepy coastal byway, I could feel a sense of enthusiasm and that this moment couldn't happen fast enough. Reminiscent of those Christmas mornings waiting for the house to awake from its sleepy slumber, all the while wanting to open presents. Here I was, despite the circumstances elated. The warmth of the sun smiled on my face and the churn of the waves gently tantalised my ears with its rhythmic movement. I could see why my dad had chosen to retire here. The salty air, gentle breeze and loud billowing from a distant pelican awoke my senses to my surroundings.

Let me digress for a moment to explain something about 'a pocket full of sunshine'. For me, this phrase personifies three things:

An attitude that develops courage.

An action that you share with others.

A feeling that describes being present to the good to great moments.

At the dawn of each new day, we have an opportunity to reset, start over and get present to life in the now. We also have a chance to turn stumbling blocks into stepping stones. To sit in joy and vitality of life. The BE's of life BE GRATEFUL, BE POSITIVE, BE PRESENT, BE YOU, BE AWARE, BE KNOWING THAT LIFE IS WORTH IT.

This was my moment as I drove to the hospital. I had spent my life developing my courage and bravery. My time had come to summon my courageous action in the wilderness of life. This wilderness was blanketed with an enormous dose of gratitude and love for a stoic, strong, strictly loving family person, my dad. As I entered the room donned with a mask, gloves, white PPE from head to toe, I saw him in a much different light.

He was frail, weakened energy, slimmer than I remember, vulnerable but still a man with every wit fighting to be here, here with me and his grandson. My heart felt his longing as his eye glistened. I took off my mask and with that first ray of hope, gently kissed his cheek. The tendrils of my heart sighed with relief to be present to this man, my dad for an entire three hours with such gladness.

Medical personnel had mentioned that my dad would not have much energy to do much of anything. Knowing my dad's brilliance, now I arrived with his grandson Joshua, he was determined to make the most of it. That smirk of prideful elation said it all. We talked, we laughed, we reminisced, we did those things that only he and I would know how to do. It was not a state of idle chatter, but rather a life fulfilment of energy exchange where love was spoken.

We shared our deepest thoughts, feelings and understandings of each other. I whispered all and everything a little girl seeing her dad for the last time would want to say. He in turn, as the loving father he was, declared with kind-heartedness everything he wanted and needed to say. Holding hands in the quiet, we knew our affection and love would not die with his last words. My dad knew well enough my capacity to be courageous and use that energy to make things happen. He tenderly shared his last wish and that I would help him make it happen. He was right, I was his girl who would bring hope and the very fulfilment of his wish.

When you are diagnosed with cancer and given days to live, certain aspects of life become very clear. Do not sweat the small stuff and get presents for those you love. My dad's deep knowing rumbled with a love for my mum that transcended past his pain and suffering. His wish was to spend a timeless, fond, sensitive moment in the arms of the only woman he ever loved and adored, my mum. The most significant seconds, minutes and hours on the clock of his life were about to unfold with my help.

Theirs was a love story that stood the test of time. Married for fifty-three years, they came together vastly different but the same in purpose and love. They understood what it meant to belong, truly belong, to themselves first and then each other. Never compromising, giving up who they were, respectively. In the beauty of their coastal home, as sure as the waves rippled, my dad's wish was fulfilled. Forever intertwined, lost in time, find the strength of each other's arms to get though the missing, the lonely and feel nothing but an eternal bond of love beyond what the human eye can see.

There is nothing more sobering to consider than what I am about to say, as I kissed my dad goodbye, I saw and felt his struggle to keep the tears from coming. With laughter I loved him back. However, underneath that spirited chuckle, I realised, *How do I walk out of this room, his room, knowing I am saying goodbye forever?* You do as I did and live in the moment with love in abundance, not dwelling on what is to come, but ever vigilant on the now, one foot in front of the other, with courage. My positive pivot of gratitude was that I had such a glorious time without limitation between us and that I created the opportunity for his last life's wish to be fulfilled, which eased a deep longing.

Goodbyes of all kinds are hard. Finding the words and emotions to say goodbye matter in such tender happenings, especially when I knew a door was about to close, meaning a huge life change was about to show up.

On the morning of the day I left, a deep knowing came and groaned like an empty tummy. It is there, and you know it. This gnawed at my heartstrings. Leaving Dad was the most difficult gruelling task ahead of me. Returning to Sydney was not a choice I could control and in truth that equalled – never seeing my dad again, ever. How do you reconcile yourself with that? Everything was coming together all at once like the repetitious vibration of a gong.

With every fibre of my soul and being I knew I was being pulled to go back to the hospital to see Dad one last time. I would not be able to do that. Forever grateful I received three wonderful hours with Dad. Dad had done something very loving, special and expelled every last ounce of energy to be with me and Joshua (my oldest son).

Inside the deep misty-grey sadness of knowing this was truly goodbye, brought reminiscent memories of twenty-seven years earlier when I left home to move to Sydney. That was my last difficult goodbye. Only this time was not about missing home, but coming back would mean that Dad was not where I could see or hear him physically, and my heart ached ferociously. I would not ever see him for the rest of my life. My heart stung with sadness but also felt deep gratitude for the time we shared together. A time well spent; memories weaved that would carry me through what was ahead of me.

As I sat on the plane with my son in silence, I looked out the window and watched the clouds drift delicately through time. My mind was reflecting on the time spent, no words could be spoken, just quiet solitude of prayer and reflection. In my reflection I saw my life, my dad and hoped for added courage and understanding of the next steps instinctively I knew would come.

Time and knowing caught up with me a week later, as I watched via a video call my father in his last moments of life. The hardest part was not his passing, it was not being able to be there to comfort and console him, to hold his hand. To send him to a resting place with all the courage

I could muster, just as he had done for me the week earlier. The empty consumed me as I felt numb and helpless to have that strength – it is like asking you not to breathe or say I love you.

COVID-19 restrictions kept me from being at his funeral. I sat in the lounge room with my husband and children feeling like a distant stranger watching the service via Zoom. One cannot imagine the listless, unsettled state of being you feel when you cannot be present to say a final goodbye.

Despite the pain and loss, I felt my dad had given me what it takes to rise up and be positive. That was until life threw me yet another challenge. Just eight months later, on 23 June 2022, it was a normal morning, chatting with family getting ready for work and the day. Jordan was out swimming. Everything was completely normal, and we had no idea what catastrophic tragedy was hurtling towards us. It was as if a huge meteor was about to impact the earth and there was nothing we could do to change the trajectory of this. It was going to arrive.

I said goodbye to my husband, Aidan, and went off to the studio to work. Behind the scenes at home, Aidan was meeting with a work colleague and Jordan was studying in his room. Aidan, not feeling well, said to his business colleague he needed to go upstairs to rest. At the prompting of Aidan's colleague, Jordan ran upstairs to check on him, only to find his dad in a full seizure.

Transition back to the studio, I was doing what I do every day, full energy, smiles and positivity. In the studio, there was no reception on anyone's phone. Meaning I was not contactable all day. As I left, I checked my phone. I was surprised and shocked there were thirty-seven missed calls. A couple of those calls were two of my husband's best friends and my two eldest sons, Joshua and Jordan. My intuition antenna went into overload. Why would they be calling and what has gone wrong?

Quickly with shaking fingers, in lightning speed went through the messages. There were numerous from Jordan, repeatedly saying *S O S*

Emergency, Please help me. Please answer. Going immediately into hyperdrive, I dialled my son, and the conversation began with, 'Where are you?' I answered. Next, with seemingly no oxygen in my body and panic overcoming me, I stammered to ask what had happened.

The next words paralysed my emotions, and the world began to spin in slow motion. Those words echoed, over and over, 'Dad had some kind of fit and the doctor's said he is not likely to survive. How quickly can you get here?' It became very surreal, very quickly.

My world was imploding. How could this be happening? I stopped being aware, not even sure how I found myself in the emergency room because it was all so surreal. Blankness mesmerised me, my mind only to be woken up as I entered the ER door to be greeted by my sons, my husband's friends and doctors who ushered me into a room to say goodbye.

The moments ticked by slowly as I was brought up to speed on what had happened that afternoon. In due course the medical team quietly and with haste ushered our little family into the intensive care room where Aidan lay. I was not prepared for what I saw, and my heart sank in despair at all the monitors that were plugged into him. So many that I was overwhelmed and yet there he was, laying there completely lifeless as if he were not even present in body or mind. I caught my breath, my body shuddered at what I was witnessing. *This cannot be happening,* I told myself, holding back the tears. *This is not happening.*

While I stared at his motionless body, the doctors were sharing procedurally what was about to happen as if it was an everyday occurrence. What you have to understand at this point, later I discovered this is something that happens every day for lots of families. They were going to bore a hole in Aidan's head to release the pressure from a major hemorrhagic stroke.

This was going to be a huge life-or-death gamble and as I stood there still stunned, I realised that for my boys, my eldest and middle, they could say goodbye, however what about my youngest son who is at school? How does he lose out, potentially missing the opportunity to say goodbye to his dad? The dice had been rolled and we had no choice, the house was losing fast and time was not on our side, we had to relieve the pressure in the most vulnerable section of the brain, the base of the skull. This was not encouraging news for our family.

Aidan had lost all primary functionality, blinking, swallowing, breathing, every single part of his body just forgot how to work. It was like someone turned the switch off and forgot to turn it back on. Again, the surreal was sinking in slowly. The boys and I left the hospital, panic stricken and filled with sadness. We were heading home to break the news to my youngest son, who would be home from school and was just fifteen years of age.

As I entered my bedroom, a place where we shared our most special moments, as I gazed around our sanctuary, it looked more like a triage hospital room with medical paraphernalia stringed from one end to the other. I quickly realised this is not a dream, this is real, very real and he may not come back here again.

When the storms of my reality subsided in the safety and confines of home I saw the devastating debris, mental, emotional and physical tolls that took place on everyone. We needed comfort and solace that all would be well. The questions came, the wondering over and over. No answers followed because there were none. I realised I was in the middle of a huge aftermath, and it had brought me to my knees. I was weakened but not broken. Listen to that for a moment – weakened but not broken.

I mustered courageous strength to offer up with my son a prayer to the divine goodness of God. Hopeful, thankful, afraid and yet there was a knowing of, *We are going to get through this, I am going to get through this.* I did not know how and in that serene peace flicker of time found the words to ask for and know what to do. My faith expanded, in action, tears streaming down my cheeks I knew small and mighty miracles would come.

Over time small miracles would be witnessed, even as soon as two days after surgery, two of my boys and I watched Aidan reach out to hold our youngest's hand. These small and simple gestures or movements brought tremendous hope to our family. Gradually, Aidan would improve to the point of being placed in a rehabilitation unit where communication got creative. Eye blinking morse code, charades, guessing whatever it would take to encourage conversation. Conversation brought a sense of togetherness.

Having a strong heart and immense courage is a gift, and through all this it was mine. Being a mum of teenage boys comes with its fair share of heart-stopping instances. Those times where split-second reaction is needed because they fall out of a something, onto something, get into things. There is never a moment when you do not worry. A week after Aidan's stroke, Jordan my middle son, went back to Hawaii. Initially there were no concerns, in fact, relief away from the chaos, away from the stress. My focus was on Aidan and his recovery.

I know for some of you reading this you may think how you find a pocket full of sunshine, gratitude, strength and courage. Before I answer that question, in an unfair tragic twist of faith, my toughest challenge was still yet to come the ultimate test of my mettle, courage, faith and hope.

A new storm on my horizon was destined to wipe out all that I had left. Jordan called and his words rang of deep concern. I calmly said, 'What is up?' Jordan then said, 'Mum, are you sitting down? I am in the hospital in Hawaii.' In my usual motherly reaction, I immediately I thought he had fallen off his bike or jumped off a ledge and hurt himself. I retorted back, 'Jesus, what have you done now?' A pause ensued, quiet and with shaky certainty, Jordan answered softly. 'Mum, I have been diagnosed with cancer and I need surgery.'

My greatest concern was the wellbeing of my son. As a woman, the ultimate dilemma had occurred. How, as a loving wife do I nurture my husband who is on life support here in Australia, at the same time be the caring, supportive mother and be by my son's side in Hawaii? I remember thinking, *I am only one person and right now I need the strength of ten.* I remember saying to myself, *I cannot do this.* In that instance I knew that I had no other choice. *Get up and get on with it,* rang loud.

As the days passed since that period of time, I have wondered how I found centre ground in such demonstrative storms. There are many inspiring words framed around storms.

'BE THE CALM OR BE THE STORM,' and 'AFTER THE STORM COMES THE CALM.' I know that I cannot change or control the outcomes. What I can control is my reaction to those grey-filled, dark billowing clouds that materialise. I decided and chose to be the calm and the light for myself and others. You need to learn to articulate what you need, even if that means telling those around you that you need time to figure it out.

When riding in the eye of the storm, I found that 'sitting in it' helped me to get clarity. Taking a break, pausing, understanding the emotions behind it all. May I add this caution regarding 'sitting in it', please understand it is not a space or way of being where you get drenched or caught up in the drama. It is just that, sitting in it, assessing emotions, needs and what you understand long enough that you get noticeably clearer on the next steps.

Knowing how to turn the wheel from a negative to a positive has become an important aspect of how I work through the middle of the storm. If you cannot change what has arrived in your space, give yourself the grace to make the most of it. I have felt those moments and found that the gold and wealth is in taking the courage to shift my perspective and make the most of what I have in the moment. What I have is a beautiful family that needs me as a pillar of strength, courage, gratitude and positivity.

In the now, I have found my commitment to discover the pockets full of sunshine. It may be as simple as Aidan, blinking, telling me that he heard me. OR it could be a story I am reporting that inspires me to find a way to share a smile with another.

Writing my story is about the legacy I choose to touch lives for good. To share life upon life, seeing in the daily mirror, value of who you are from the inside out one moment, one day at a time. I hope that each sentence, paragraph and page has lifted you up with every turn. I hope that you found your pocket full of sunshine in these words today and will move forward with renewed intention to find your own pockets of sunshine.

KAREN LEDBURY
Tv Host / Media Personality / Key Note Speaker
Connect: @karenledbury

ANGELICA BRIDGES
YOU CAN TAKE THE GIRL OUT OF THE SMALL TOWN BUT YOU CAN'T TAKE THE SMALL TOWN OUT OF THE GIRL

I grew up in a small town in Missouri, USA, and consider myself pretty down to earth because of that. My childhood was reminiscent of one of those strong-willed, wild at heart and adventurous protagonis's you read about in a Mark Twain novel.

Though I have travelled and lived in other parts of the world and have had some truly extraordinary and fascinating life experiences since leaving that small town many years ago, I have been able to stay well grounded. After moving from a slow-paced lifestyle to the bright lights of LA after high school, I was able to learn how to be a chameleon as needed and adapt to an array of environments. I will always 'make the best' of whatever situation I find myself in. Because of this versatile nature, it has made even the worst-case scenarios I have found myself in a little more bearable. I am grateful for being raised in a non-cosmopolitan area. It gave me a softer outlook and respect for the simpler things in life. When you have found satisfaction in spending a whole day happily skipping rocks on a lake or pond and can get completely immersed in the patterns of the little waves that they create, it's not surprising I prefer some 'green acres' over a concrete jungle.

EARLY IMPRESSIONS AFFECT YOUR FUTURE SELF

I do think I was born to do what I do in life and that I am here for a special calling, no doubt about that. I have an unwavering faith in God and believe that there is a higher power and an unfathomable love that created us, above all. I also credit my ability to do what I do and confidence to do it to being blessed with 'salt of the earth' parents. Although my parents were strict while I was growing up, I was raised in 'faith' and had a family that never broke my spirit and supported my ideas and quests no matter how ridiculous they may have seemed to the average person. From an early age I was bound and determined to go out into the world and conquer my dreams. I would literally tell my parents daily what *they* needed to do in order for me to do just that. For instance, I would call and sign myself up for dance lessons, pageants, show choir, plays, summer camps, cheerleading, charm school, sports leagues, junior fashion boards and volunteer work and then I would let them know about it afterwards. I would just tell them where I needed to be and what time I needed to be there. They made sure I never left a stone I was seeking unturned. My mother would make sure to drop whatever she was doing and get me wherever I needed to be and supported me beyond belief. I could be a little rebellious and questioned everything. I was quite tenacious and argued my positions so eloquently, that my parents got that I was on a mission and they were kind of along for the ride! I have such a deep respect and unfathomable love for them because of that. I would watch them as well and learned by their actions that with hard work and believing in what you do, you can truly create the life that you want. Sounds a bit cliché, but they were fabulous role models in their unique and individual ways. I observed how disciplined and hardworking they were coming from humble beginnings. I saw how they were always helping other people and giving their time and resources. I grew up thinking that everyone was like this. I didn't know any different. I really got lucky with the early foundation. Now, my family may not have believed I was going to go out to Hollywood and get on a popular TV show that would go on to be in the Guinness World Records as 'The Most Watched TV Show in the World', but they for sure never let me know that! It's amazing how as children we absorb a lot from our parents, caregivers and teachers. It's not even so much of what they 'tell' us, but by their actions that have the most impact. Just a powerful reminder now as a parent, that my daughters are also watching me and will subconsciously take in my journey as their subliminal road map as well.

TASMANIAN DEVILS ALSO COME FROM THE MIDWEST

My favourite memories were those of simplicity, being outdoors and having a special love and bond with animals that was quite profound. I grew up as an energetic, creative, fiery and sensitive youngster with a mane of red hair and skinny legs. I preferred being barefoot any day to having to wear shoes. My dad's nickname for me was 'Tasmanian Devil' which came from one of his favourite cartoons, *Bugs Bunny*. The Tasmanian devil in the cartoon was nothing like the actual ones that come from Australia. The cartoon version would come into a room going 100mph and ignite it with his wild energy and tornado-like physicality. I thought it was hilarious and it only inspired me to give my best running into the room like a class-five storm impression whenever I could. I loved to make people laugh and enjoyed coming up with new pranks and embarrassing my mother – especially at the mall. In front of other shoppers, I would run up to a mannequin and start performing a scene that I had seen on a soap opera with an over-the-top kiss, just to watch my mom turn absolutely beet red and run out of the store. I definitely wasn't afraid to put myself out there. Another reason why I enjoy doing improv and comedic roles in acting more than others. Comedy is my forte. Maybe the desire for comedy also acts as an 'escape' from the serious issues in life. I find laughter to be very healing. Also, when I am laughing, it automatically puts me 'in the present moment'. Your attention is brought to whatever is giving you the joyful physical and mental sensations to respond. It's not always easy to be 'present', but when we laugh, we truly are! Not to mention it strengthens our immune system and releases dopamine and endorphins, which are those fabulous feel-good hormones. I'll take as many of those as I can get, thank you.

RURAL ROOTS

During my younger days, we lived on a dirt/gravel road with a three-digit number address that had an RR in front of it. The RR stood for 'Rural Route'. Later on, we moved into the 'city limits', but living on the ranch out in the country were some of the most impressionable years now looking back. We were out there. So far out, that my dad had a gas pump installed over by the barn and the gas fill-up truck would come once a month or whatever it was to fill up the underground tank, so we would have our own gas without having to drive super far to get it . One day my father came home with a new buggy (as in horse and buggy). It seated four people quite comfortably. We would hook up one of our horses to it and my sister, my parents and I would take these buggy rides. We would do this at least once a week and it became our family bonding type of sunset/dusk outing. We were definitely giving *Little House on the Prairie* a run for its money when we would cruise around in that thing on those back roads.

OLD-SCHOOL

Being in a town with a population of 150 people in my early elementary days meant small school. A small school in a rural countryside also came with what I call nowadays 'old-school' procedures. This neck of the woods wasn't even classified as a 'village' since from what I understand a village usually has a minimum of five hundred inhabitants. There were six kids in my first-grade class. One day we were instructed to do an art project in class using Elmer's glue and Cheerios. The assignment was to glue the individual Cheerios any way you wanted onto the piece of construction paper to create your 'art'. After we were done making our creation, we put our art paper on the windowsill to dry on a Friday. On Monday we came back to school and the art projects had dried. I don't know why, but the dried glued Cheerios on Matthew's art looked so irresistible and I guess maybe I was hungry. I ended up pulling every Cheerio off his paper and eating it. Dried glue and all. When it was time for Matthew to get up in front of the class and talk about what he made and why he did, his project was blank except for some lingering glue spots from where the cereal had been stuck to it. The good news is that I felt bad because of my moment of weakness, and I admitted to eating his project. The bad news is, when you stepped out of line at this school you got the paddle – aka corporal punishment. I remember watching the principal come down the hall with black pants, shiny black patent leather shoes and his white short-sleeved button-up shirt with a ballpoint pen attached to his shirt pocket. His hair was slicked back with a significant amount of Brylcreem (a sight even Elvis Presley would have been envious of) carrying the dreaded black spanking paddle. The penalty for this Cheerio infringement would be one swat on the bum. It was done outside the class in the hallway, and I had to bend over so the principal could have a good contact point. After that swat of the paddle, it was right back into the classroom and back to business as usual. These days, if a student 'destroyed' another student's creation, the teacher would say in an overly syrupy voice, 'Angie, now use your words and tell Matthew what motivated you to eat his project.' And then the syrupy tone would say to Matthew, 'Now, Matthew, use your words to tell Angie how that made you feel to come back to school and find your artwork eaten.' That is exactly how it would have gone down, at least in California, I think it probably would. Not where I'm from. Different times too. The good thing is that I never ate someone's 'artwork' ever again. I have the most respect ever for other people's art and … I still LOVE me some Cheerios.

Now, while I am on the subject of old-fashioned cruel and unusual punishment, I will touch on the downside of 'country neighbours'. The further out you are, the further some folks like to push rules, restrictions, and sometimes, human decency. My sister and I had a pet goat (surprisingly) named Billy. Billy was like a six-year-old kid. We had the same Tasmanian devil thing going with the boundless amounts of energy. He loved playing chase and freeze tag with us and would keep us entertained for hours on end. He was super intelligent. He could also cuddle when he would get tired. I would go out to the barn and read all of my books to him. Many nights my mom would have to call out to the barn for me to come in because it was so late and so dark out there. There were so many times I contemplated sneaking Billy inside the house to hang out with me and sleep in my room. I wish I would have. One morning, I woke to my sister screaming and crying. Something had happened to Billy. He was missing. She had overhead my parent's conversation about some 'neighbours' and a wild party and a BBQ down the dirt road. I was not supposed to hear any of this, but of course my sister burst into my room telling me that one of the neighbours had come and stolen our precious Billy from the barn and … had made him the main dish for their BBQ. I guess my dad intuitively knew they had done something nefarious with all of the hooting and hollering all night and went over there the next morning and saw the remnants of my 'bestie' over their fire which was now just a heap of ashes. I was devastated, horrified and inconsolable. This was the beginning of when I realised how deep my attachment to animals really went. I couldn't believe something like this could even happen. I mourned that goat, which seemed like forever. I mean, didn't they know how much I loved that little guy? Some of the downsides to living in the boonies is that you can have neighbours that also happen to be barbarians. Not long after that incident we moved. We still lived in the area but put some distance between us and those monsters down the lane.

IF I COULD ONLY BOTTLE THIS AND PUT IT IN A JAR

As having had some heartbreak with the death of my first pet, happier moments were spent catching frogs and tadpoles by day and lightning bugs by night. Summer days were spent climbing trees and playing in creeks and cornfields and winter ones were sliding on our UFO-resemblant silver sleds across the ice on the lake or down the snowy embankments. Baking and canning vegetables alongside my grandmother and getting the goodies out of the garden were highlights. I would carry whatever veggies or fruit in the bottom of my shirt which I had made into a makeshift bowl. Making homemade jams from plum trees and blackberry bushes started an affection for culinary that dominates me even more today. Especially the concept of ‹food only tastes as good as the love you put into it’ ingrained in my DNA. I also loved swimming in our lake and floating around in a big ol’ tractor tyre inner tube. Forget those silly fancy pink swans that litter pools these days; these are the best flotation devices, btw. Sleeping with the dogs in ‹their’ dog house outside was a regular sleepover for me. I wanted to be closer to them and had an indescribable understanding and love for them. I truly love any and every kind of animal and got a horse I named Big Red. I was the ‘little red’ and he was the big one. I was always surrounded by cattle, cats, dogs, horses, rabbits and the occasional rescue opossum. Of course, Billy the goat will always be in my heart. Being right in the middle of nature was like breathing oxygen for me.

WHAT DID WE DO BEFORE CELLPHONES?! CREATE! CREATE! CREATE!

All this reminiscence of how I grew up brings me to a very important subject. How beautiful it was to not have technology at our fingertips or social media shadowing every single thing we did. When people now say, 'What did we do before cellphones and social media!?' – I'll tell you what we did … we LIVED, and to the fullest. We explored and used our imagination and connected with people, our environment and animals on a level that we don't even have anymore. Because we have thousands of images and streams of entertainment thrown at us, we don't need to use our imaginations as much – at least this is what I have observed. All this stimulating content is being fed to us and at lightning speed. That part of our mind and brain that comes into this world as an untouched place of pure creativity is overstimulated with other people's posts, experiences and influence. I really miss those simpler days of having to create my own entertainment. This brings me to the fact that I am so happy to have experienced a childhood that I didn't know any better but to dream, create, invent, make-believe and inspire myself on a daily basis. No-one was going to do it for me. I was much more creative then than I am now.

BIG FISH IN A LITTLE POND

As I got into my teens, I continued to do just that. I eased out of sports and started to focus entirely on theatre, singing, modelling and writing. Little did I know, when I turned eighteen, I would set out on a mission to make my way right into the hypnotic arms and charms of Hollywood, by trading in that laid-back, suburbia reality to a larger-than-life one. It was time. I started to feel like an alien in that small town. Even though I loved it, it began to constrict me and I felt for the first time that there was a ceiling above me. This little guppy was blossoming into a sailfish. I knew I needed to jump out of that little pond and make it to the ocean before I ran out of air. It wasn't a bad thing. It was just that my con-science became aware that it wanted more, needed more and wouldn't be fulfilled until it was able to experience more. I was ready to travel the world, experience different cultures, experience the'"big city' life and use my God-given talent to perform and create. This was the beginning of my professional and life-changing journey.

THE SUPERHERO COMPLEX AND OTHER UNATTAINABLE ARCHETYPES

Your health is your wealth. The one thing that has truly tested me was when I was involved in an auto accident, and I was hit from behind by a distracted driver on a busy freeway in Los Angeles during rush hour. Being such a healthy and vibrant person, my entire life I never had to deal with any truly debilitating health issues before. My name is Angelica and I have a superhero complex. Some people relate to archetypes. There are different types that have been used in history and used to describe characteristics of humans as well. It's also kinda cool just to look at these created archetypes and see which ones you resonate with. I haven't really studied them too deeply, but I know if I were going to assign an archetype to myself, the first would be superhero/superheroine. I consider myself someone that enjoys helping others. I want to give my service, be there to rescue people and animals, be physically capable, always, and I have always considered myself just a total unbreakable, strong, resilient being. Hey, I'm immortal and nothing is ever gonna stop me. With that being said, I did walk away from that accident, saying, 'Oh, I'm fine, I'm fine.' Obviously, as time went by my body had another plan and opinion. I struggled with so many symptoms and neurological issues that were difficult to treat. I think when you are so used to being filled with so much vitality and gusto, and we have something that then physically changes the ability to function at the level that we were used to functioning, it can affect us profoundly. I looked great on the outside which only made all the neurologists and specialists not know where to start. Internally, was a whole other level. For once, I was forced to stop and listen to my body. I had so many questions and was beyond frustrated. For once in my life, this was not really something I had any control over. Sadly, the very skills that I was used to abiding by that 'if I worked harder and faster, did the right thing in life, and continued to use my God-given talent' wasn't really going to give me too much relief in this situation. I was also just so used to being a superhero and not showing weakness. People need me. Animals need me. I don't have one minute I can be down. The biggest surprise to me, above everything, was that I could NOT get my head around the fact that most – and I will say roughly nine out of the ten – specialists and doctors that I saw just wanted to prescribe medication for the symptoms and be done. Again, I had not had much experience with injuries or illnesses, so this was mind-blowing to me. How can anyone take an oath in the medical/health field and just prescribe pills to people every day? If I spent all of those years in medical school, I would absolutely care and want to heal every single person that came to me and try and get to the root of their problem! I don't want to treat symptoms; I want to go straight to the origin and understand why it is out of balance or not functioning. Understandably, some people need medication to live, balance a deficiency or prolong their life. I get that. But, for other ailments, how about taking the time to figure out the root of the issue, so you don't have to prescribe medication that's just treating a symptom? Most of the doctors didn't even try. I had no idea this was so dominant. I understand the financial factor in regards to pharmaceuticals. It was still eye-opening nonetheless.

That time period really made me start to think about what is most important in life and how and who my energy should be given to accordingly. How I spend my time is even more precious to me. There are so many things in life I want to do and finish and complete that I haven't even done yet. I have so many ideas and so many dreams and so many aspirations. I needed for a moment to put down that notion that I always have to be the strongest in the room and that I have to be the one to take care of everybody around me. My body was telling me it's time to slow down, re-evaluate the crucial things and most importantly it was to just listen to my body. It needed physical therapy and rest. It was hard for me to digest, but I knew that if I wanted to do all of those things that I still needed to do, I had to go through healing, but on my body's schedule. I surrendered to that and began to listen; yet without giving up. Once I did that, I just got stronger each day and I was able to heal and feel like myself again. Most importantly, I realised I don't always have to wear my cape. At the end of the day it is all about balance and important to keep the mind, body and your soul fed equally.

LIFE ISN'T ABOUT THE CARDS YOU ARE DEALT, BUT HOW YOU PLAY THE CARDS IN LIFE

You know the old saying, 'It's not so much about the cards that we have been dealt with in life but the way we see those cards and how we play them.'

Our state of mind and wellbeing really depends on how we interpret what happens to us. Going through life being a victim of circumstances is not going to bring or attract anything other than the exact label of being a 'victim' and not being able to get out of it. I've felt plenty of that *I can't believe this has happened to me!* The more I felt like I had been targeted or taken advantage of the more I seemed to attract these same scenarios over and over. Funny how that works. If that doesn't tell you how powerful your thoughts are and words you tell yourself or others, try thinking only good things for a whole day and then do the next day where you just focus on everything negative. It's quite poetic how the universe listens and gives you more of what you focus on.

I have experienced the death of loved ones and precious pets. I went through a divorce (which some people say can affect you the same way). I have had betrayal, a multitude of disappointments and losses. When I first moved to California, I was mugged in an underground parking structure in a mall as I got into my convertible. They were two escaped convicts from a nearby prison that tried tying my hands to the steering wheel with a rope so they could grab all of my things without resistance. Well, that didn't work. They had no idea they had tried to mug a Tasmanian devil. LOL. There goes my 'superhero' fight-or-flight response – again. I fought hard and got loose, and crazily enough, I tried chasing one of them. I didn't catch them, but thankfully for me, it may have been a much different scenario. I would not recommend chasing robbers, but I would not have done anything differently. Actually, I did it again when my car was getting stolen in the middle of the night twenty years later. I ran out and confronted car thieves in my driveway. I am a light sleeper and heard clinking outside. By the time I hit the yard running, they had hot-wired our car and were screeching out of the driveway. I then just made a little call to ONSTAR and had the vehicle shut down. It had only gotten one mile away, so they did not get very far. I also got the vehicle back. Again, I do not recommend confronting criminals. I just do not want to be anyone's 'victim'. Straight up. If you stay in a victim mindset, you will keep attracting situations that continue to put you as a weak being that has no control over what happens to them or the reaction to it. I learned to use the very things that I felt were the most painful, uncomfortable and challenging to learn from and rise above. If something has been painful and hard for me, I let myself acknowledge the obvious and then I have trained myself to then feel it's okay to feel this, but now let's see how we can rise from this and be and feel even better. I've found that I can come out of a dark or negative place even quicker when I use that very depth to catapult and empower me. I've used it to ignite a spark in my soul to want to be better, to make things better and to make difficult changes. Sometimes it's hard for us to change unless we are moved deeply by something and if we're not able to change, grow or adjust, we can't really evolve. Stagnation is boring. Life is not going to be easy, but I also understand most suffering is quite temporary in the grand scheme of things – I just want to grow. I just want to be better than I was yesterday. Is that possible? I don't know, but all I know is that I feel more wise and I can be more conscious of others and their experiences and their feelings. I can be a better listener. I can be a better friend and be a better parent. I seem to navigate my life much more strategically when I've taken the very things that I thought I wouldn't be able to make it through and learn from them and grow from them and be a better person because of them.

LESSONS AND BLESSINGS – THEY ARE REALLY THE SAME THING

I always try to ask myself, *What is the lesson in this circumstance?* I have learned now from all of my experiences that there is always a bigger picture to anything and everything. Sometimes when we are coming from an 'emotional' perspective it's hard to see it. With enough stillness and openness to the lesson or the blessing that will come, there will always be some kind of gift that awaits. It could be a subtle gesture or an earth-shaking one. Now I look back on all challenges and I am grateful for whatever I went through. I see that I am also even more compassionate after having climbed so many mountains. I know I can hang up my superhero cape once in a while and take a break from trying to save the things that are out of my control. I am able now to just bless those that I felt had harmed me or I was indifferent to. I bless the situations that at one point had me down on my knees not knowing if I could go on another minute. It's so freeing to release, forgive and move on as needed. I just want to feed my soul positively. When I welcome the lessons and send out even more blessings. I'm doing just that.

ANGELICA BRIDGES

Tv Host / Producer / Philanthropist / Founder of Angelicakitchen

Connect: angelicabridgesofficial.com / @angelicabridges

CATAREEYA MARSDEN
FROM SILENCE TO STRENGTH: A JOURNEY OF SELF-DISCOVERY

The decision to uproot my life at the age of thirteen and move from the vibrant city of Bangkok to the unfamiliar land of Florida was a pivotal moment in my story. As a young girl on the cusp of adolescence, I had never anticipated such a drastic change, especially one that would separate me from everything and everyone I had known.

The news of the move came abruptly, leaving me without a say in the matter. It was a decision made by my mother, who believed that this new environment would provide better opportunities for my education and future. While I understood her intentions were rooted in love and concern, I couldn't help but feel a sense of helplessness and uncertainty.

As I bid farewell to my familiar surroundings, my heart felt heavy with the weight of leaving behind my friends, my school and the life I had known. The language barrier posed an additional challenge, as I did not speak English fluently. The prospect of starting afresh in a foreign land felt overwhelming, and a sense of isolation began to take hold.

Upon arriving in Florida, I found myself in the care of my aunt, a woman with whom I had never formed a close bond. Her parenting style starkly contrasted with that of my mother, and our relationship was characterised by a sense of detachment. As she navigated the complexities of integrating her own son into her newly formed family, my presence became an afterthought – an extra responsibility in an already busy household.

In those initial years, I struggled to find my place in this new world. The outgoing, confident girl I had once been seemed to fade away, replaced by a shell of caution and reticence. The language barrier and cultural differences left me feeling like an outsider, unable to fully connect with my peers. Loneliness became my constant companion, and I sought solace in the company of a younger girl next door, who became my closest friend during those formative years.

While I gradually adapted to my new surroundings, mastering the English language and forming a circle of acquaintances, something within me had shifted. The experiences of isolation and feeling unheard had left a lasting impact. I had learned to keep my thoughts to myself, to hide behind a facade of silence, fearing ridicule or judgement for my accent and differences.

The lively, chatty girl had become a wallflower – a master at blending into the background, avoiding attention and confrontation. I had become adept at moulding myself into the image of a 'good girl', seeking validation and approval from others rather than embracing my true self.

This phase of my life was filled with significant changes and the need to adjust to new circumstances. It was a time of loss and longing, as I yearned for the connection and sense of belonging I had left behind. Yet, even in the midst of this uncertainty, seeds of resilience and determination were sown within me.

After finally finding a sense of belonging in Florida, life seemed to be unfolding beautifully for me. I had adapted to the bustling energy of the city, made cherished friendships and immersed myself in the rich cultural diversity that surrounded me. My dream of pursuing a university education in the United States felt like it was within reach, and I couldn't have been more excited about the possibilities that lay ahead.

However, fate had a different path in store for me. Just when I had settled into this new-found sense of belonging, the Asian economy took an unexpected nosedive. The financial crisis that followed sent shockwaves through the global economy, leaving no corner untouched, including my dreams of studying in the US.

As an international student, I had always been aware of the higher cost of attending college compared to American citizens, but the economic downturn magnified the financial burden to an overwhelming extent. The cost of tuition and living expenses soared to exorbitant heights, nearly two to three times higher than what my American peers would pay. It was a harsh reality that shattered my plans, leaving me feeling disheartened and lost in the midst of uncertainty. Adding to the weight of this financial struggle was the knowledge that my mother, a single mom who had always worked tirelessly to support my education, would bear the brunt of these expenses. The thought of the cost being too much for her and the sacrifices she would have to make weighed heavily on my mind, intensifying the sense of responsibility I felt to find a solution.

The news of the financial crisis hit me like a tidal wave, and I found myself grappling with a whirlwind of emotions. Disappointment, frustration and a deep sense of injustice swirled within me as I faced the harsh truth that my dream of a US university education might not become a reality after all.

I had always believed in the power of education and the opportunities it could unlock. To me, studying in the United States represented a chance to broaden my horizons, engage with diverse perspectives and gain a world-class education that could propel me toward my aspirations. It was a dream that I had nurtured for years, and now it felt like it was slipping through my fingers.

As the reality of the situation settled in, I faced a challenging crossroad. Should I let go of my dream and pursue alternative paths in my home country? Should I put my education on hold and wait for more stable times? The uncertainty weighed heavily on me, and I found myself searching for answers amidst the chaos of the economic downturn.

But amidst the cloud of uncertainty, a flicker of determination ignited within me. I refused to be defeated by the circumstances beyond my control. I knew that giving up on my dreams was not an option; I had come too far and worked too hard to let them slip away now.

Driven by my unwavering belief in education's power, I began to explore alternative pathways. I delved into research, seeking out scholarships, grants and financial aid opportunities that could help alleviate the burden of the exorbitant costs. I reached out to university counsellors and sought guidance from mentors, eager to discover any glimmer of hope that would allow me to continue my educational journey.

In the face of adversity, I discovered a community of support. Friends, family and educators rallied behind me, offering their encouragement and assistance. Their belief in my potential fuelled my determination to overcome the obstacles in my path.

As I persevered, I realised that this setback was an opportunity to reassess my goals and priorities. While studying in the United States had been my dream, it was not the only path to success and personal growth. There were countless other avenues to explore, both in my home country and around the world.

With an open mind and a willingness to embrace change, I began exploring options closer to home. I discovered universities in Bangkok that offered diverse international programs in business, engineering and economics. While the idea of staying in my home country initially felt like a compromise, I soon realised that these programs offered unique opportunities for personal and professional development.

Choosing to focus on the possibilities that lay ahead rather than dwelling on what had been lost, I redirected my energy toward preparing for the entrance exams required for these programs. My determination to succeed was stronger than ever, and I threw myself wholeheartedly into studying and preparing for this new chapter of my educational journey.

As I navigated the process of applying for the international programs, I found myself reflecting on the experiences and growth I had gained during my time in Florida. The Sunshine State had not only provided me with a sense of belonging but had also instilled in me a deep appreciation for cultural diversity and a global perspective.

Adjusting back to life in Bangkok was not without its challenges. I felt like I was caught between the western and eastern worlds, straddling the cultural divide and seeking to find my place within it. Yet, I realised that this unique position was a strength, a gift that allowed me to bridge the gap between different cultures and perspectives.

With renewed determination and an unwavering commitment to my education, I embraced my new path with enthusiasm. Although the road ahead was different from what I had imagined, I knew that my journey was far from over. My experience of overcoming adversity and seeking alternative pathways has taught me the power of resilience, adaptability and the importance of staying true to my dreams.

As I took my first steps into the international programs at the university, I carried with me the lessons and experiences that had shaped me into the person I had become. The challenges and setbacks had tested my resolve, but they had also revealed the strength of my character and the depths of my determination.

I embraced the fusion of cultures within me, using it as a bridge to build connections with my peers and educators. I found myself not just adjusting to life in Bangkok, but thriving within the diverse and dynamic learning environment.

As I successfully graduated from university and landed a coveted position at one of the prestigious big four accounting firms, it seemed like life was unfolding exactly as planned. From an outsider's perspective, I had achieved the markers of success and accomplishment that society often equates with happiness and fulfilment. I had checked all the boxes, excelled in my studies and secured a promising career. Yet, despite these achievements, there was an unshakable feeling within me that something was missing.

The fast-paced world of accounting provided me with a sense of security and stability, but as the days turned into weeks and the weeks into months, I couldn't ignore the nagging sense of emptiness. The long hours, demanding workload and the pressure to climb the corporate ladder left little room for self-reflection. I had become so engrossed in the pursuit of success that I had lost sight of the deeper meaning and purpose behind it all.

As I immersed myself in the corporate world, I couldn't help but reflect on the dreams and passions that had once ignited a fire within me. I remembered the sense of wonder and curiosity that had driven me to explore different paths during my formative years. I had once dreamt of making a difference, of using my skills to contribute to something greater than myself, and yet, somewhere along the way, those dreams had taken a back seat to the demands of society's expectations.

In the midst of the fluorescent-lit office spaces and the buzz of business transactions, I longed for a sense of connection – to my true self and to the world around me. I yearned for a deeper meaning to my work, a purpose that would infuse each day with a sense of fulfilment and joy. The pursuit of success had led me to a crossroads, forcing me to confront the misalignment between my external achievements and the internal yearning for purpose and meaning.

In the quiet moments of introspection, I began to question the essence of true happiness. Was it merely the accumulation of accolades, material possessions and societal recognition? Or was there something more profound that lay beneath the surface, something that could only be found by reconnecting with my authentic self and the passions that had once set my soul ablaze?

The decision to embark on a journey of self-discovery was both daunting and exhilarating. I knew that I needed to break free from the confines of my familiar environment – a place where the judging eyes and constant comparison among family members seemed all too common, especially in our culture. I craved the freedom to explore my true self, away from the expectations and preconceived notions that had been placed upon me.

In my heart, I felt the pull to be alone, to distance myself from the noise of external influences and immerse myself in a space of self-reflection. It was a choice driven by a deep yearning to reconnect with the essence of who I really was and to discern what I truly wanted from life. I understood that this journey required solitude, a sacred space where I could shed the layers of external conditioning and listen to the whispers of my soul.

With unwavering determination, I decided to continue my graduate school education in Sydney, Australia – a land where I knew no-one and where I felt I could truly be myself. It was a bold step into the unknown, but I embraced it as an opportunity to explore and rediscover my authentic self.

As I embarked on this new chapter of my life, I found myself filled with a mix of excitement and trepidation. Leaving behind the familiar comforts of home and venturing into the uncharted territory of a foreign land was both liberating and nerve-wracking. However, I knew that this journey was essential for my personal growth and finding the clarity I sought.

Arriving in Sydney, I was greeted by the beauty of a new landscape, the exciting energy of a diverse city and the enchanting allure of Australian culture. It was a breath of fresh air, a canvas upon which I could paint the colours of my true self without inhibition. The absence of familiar faces allowed me to step into my own identity, free from the expectations and judgements of others.

Living in solitude, I had the freedom to explore my passions, interests and dreams without the influence of external pressures. I immersed myself in my graduate studies, choosing a field that resonated deeply with my core values and aspirations. I was no longer constrained by the limited options that had once defined my choices; instead, I embraced the opportunity to pursue a path that aligned with my true passions.

In the quiet moments of reflection, I delved into the depths of my being, peeling back the layers of conditioning that had shaped my beliefs and desires. I questioned the narratives that had been imposed upon me, reclaiming my power to define my own destiny. Each day brought new revelations as I discovered facets of myself that had been long suppressed.

As I navigated this journey of self-discovery, I found solace in the beauty of nature that surrounded me in Sydney. The vast expanse of blue skies, the crashing waves on the coastline and the serene green spaces became my sanctuaries for introspection. In these moments, I connected with the profound wisdom that resided within me, understanding that my true self was intricately woven into the fabric of the universe.

Along this transformative path, I encountered challenges and moments of doubt. The process of rediscovering oneself is not without its hurdles, and there were times when I questioned my decisions and feared the unknown. Yet, each obstacle became an opportunity for growth and resilience. I learned to trust my intuition, to embrace vulnerability and to believe in my ability to navigate through life's uncertainties.

As I embraced my individuality and learned to love myself unconditionally, I noticed a shift in my perception of the world. The judgement that had once clouded my interactions with others began to fade, replaced by empathy and a deep understanding of the unique journeys we all embark upon. I no longer felt the need to compare myself to others, recognising that we are all on our distinct paths, each beautiful in its own way.

Through this journey of self-discovery, I also forged new connections with people from diverse backgrounds and cultures. I found solace in the company of like-minded individuals who encouraged me to embrace my true self and supported my pursuit of authenticity. Together, we celebrated our uniqueness and shared the joy of growing into our most genuine selves.

Gradually, I began to integrate the various facets of my identity – the eastern and western influences that had once felt conflicting now harmoniously coexisted within me. I learned that I could embody both worlds, embracing the richness of my cultural heritage while honouring the individuality that set me apart.

Another significant hurdle I needed to overcome was my sense of self-belief. Throughout my life, I had been conditioned to seek external validation and to rely on others' opinions of me to determine my self-worth. However, I now understood that true self-belief came from within, and it was imperative to trust and believe in myself, regardless of what others thought.

In a world that often measured success and worth through external accomplishments and recognition, I made a conscious effort to shift my focus inward. I started to pay attention to my inner dialogue, becoming aware of the limiting beliefs and self-doubt that had held me back for far too long. I realised that my own thoughts and beliefs about myself were powerful, shaping not only my perceptions of the world but also influencing the actions I took.

As I delved deeper into this process of self-discovery, I confronted the negative narratives that had played on repeat in my mind. I challenged the voices that whispered, *You're not good enough*, or, *You don't deserve success.* Instead, I replaced them with affirmations that reinforced my self-worth and abilities. I reminded myself daily that I was capable, resilient and worthy of pursuing my dreams.

The road to building self-belief was not without its challenges. As I sought to break free from the chains of external validation, I faced moments of doubt and uncertainty. There were times when I wondered if I was making the right choices or if I had what it took to succeed in my new environment.

Finding a job in Sydney proved to be a particularly testing experience. The job market was competitive, and my international status added an extra layer of complexity. Despite being well-qualified, I encountered obstacles and rejections along the way. The uncertainty of job hunting made it tempting to fall back into old patterns of seeking approval from others.

However, I remained steadfast in my commitment to believing in myself. I reminded myself of the journey I had undertaken, the hurdles I had overcome and the strength I had found within. I knew that my worth was not defined by the job titles or the opinions of others – it was defined by the belief I had in my own capabilities and the passion that fuelled my desire for growth and fulfilment.

The struggle to find a suitable job led me to a role that, on paper, seemed to be far below my qualifications and potential. However, I chose to view it as an opportunity rather than a setback. I realised that this position could serve as a stepping stone, a chance to gain valuable experience and prove to myself that I was capable of adapting and excelling in any circumstance.

Embracing this mindset allowed me to approach the job with enthusiasm and determination. I poured my heart into every task, focusing on delivering my best regardless of the role's perceived limitations. As days turned into weeks and weeks into months, I began to witness a remarkable transformation – not just in my professional abilities, but also in my sense of self-belief.

Through hard work and dedication, I proved to myself that my capabilities were not determined by external titles or labels. I had the power to shape my own narrative, and I discovered a new-found sense of confidence that transcended any job description.

This process of self-belief was not a linear journey. It involved constant self-reflection, perseverance and the willingness to embrace vulnerability. There were days when I stumbled, when doubt crept back in and when I felt the weight of external expectations. However, each time I faltered, I reminded myself of the progress I had made and the sense of empowerment I had gained.

As I continued to nurture my self-belief, I noticed a positive shift in my overall outlook on life. I became more resilient in the face of challenges, more proactive in pursuing opportunities and more accepting of my authentic self. The bamboo ceiling, which had once seemed insurmountable, began to lose its power over me. I recognised that the limits imposed by societal norms were not reflections of my abilities but were rather illusions to be shattered.

Breaking through the invisible ceiling, as a woman of colour in a traditionally male-dominated field, was a journey that required immense courage, resilience and self-assurance. It was a path that began with my decision to embark on a voyage of self-discovery in Sydney, Australia, and continued as I returned home with a new-found sense of purpose and authenticity.

As I stepped into the world of emergency services, I was keenly aware of the challenges that lay ahead. The bamboo ceiling, a subtle yet powerful barrier that hindered the progression of women and minorities in western cultures, loomed before me. It was a barrier that manifested through unconscious biases, stereotypes and preconceived notions that undermined the potential of individuals based on their gender and ethnicity.

Yet, the journey of self-discovery had armed me with a profound sense of self-assurance. I had learned to embrace my true identity, recognising the value of my unique perspective and experiences. It was this new-found self-acceptance that enabled me to confront the ingrained limitations with determination and unwavering confidence.

I knew that to break through this barrier, I had to navigate my way through a sea of scepticism and misconceptions. I was prepared to challenge the status quo and prove that competence, passion and dedication knew no boundaries of gender or race.

In my role within the emergency services agency, I strived to excel not only in my professional duties but also in my interactions with colleagues and superiors. I approached every task with diligence and a commitment to excellence, knowing that my performance would be under scrutiny. I worked tirelessly to gain the respect of my peers and demonstrate that I was just as capable, if not more so, as any of my colleagues.

As I contributed to the agency's mission and demonstrated my expertise, I began to dismantle the bamboo ceiling piece by piece. I was relentless in advocating for myself and other women of colour, encouraging equal opportunities and representation at all levels of the organisation. I sought out mentors and allies who recognised the value of diversity and inclusion, working collaboratively to drive positive change within the agency.

With time, my efforts bore fruit, and I earned a seat at the table – a place where my voice and perspectives were not only heard but valued. My journey had taught me that representation mattered, that diverse voices contributed to more comprehensive and effective decision-making processes.

In breaking through the bamboo ceiling, I became a trailblazer, setting a precedent for others who aspired to overcome barriers in their own fields. I recognised the responsibility that came with my achievements – to uplift and empower others who faced similar challenges, to inspire them to pursue their dreams unapologetically.

As I continued to excel in my role, my presence in the traditionally male-dominated field served as a catalyst for change. More women of colour began to join the agency, and a shift in organisational culture became evident. The invisible barriers that had once hindered progress were gradually eroded, and diversity became a cornerstone of the agency's identity.

Through the power of representation and an unyielding commitment to excellence, I had not only broken the bamboo ceiling in my own life but had also contributed to reshaping the culture of the emergency services agency. Today, I stand as a symbol of empowerment and a testament to the transformative power of embracing one's true self.

As I look back on my journey – from feeling lost between two worlds to confidently asserting my identity and breaking through barriers – I am filled with a sense of fulfilment and pride. My path was not easy, and the road to success was paved with obstacles, but I never lost sight of the strength that lay within me.

In the ever-changing landscape of life, I remain committed to continued growth, both personally and professionally. I acknowledge that the journey of self-discovery and breaking barriers is an ongoing process – one that requires adaptability, resilience and an unwavering commitment to authenticity.

My experiences have taught me that each of us possesses the power to challenge the status quo and redefine the narratives that govern our lives. By embracing our unique identities and forging paths of our own, we can shatter the bamboo ceilings that limit our potential and create a world where diversity and inclusivity flourish.

As I continue on my personal growth journey, I do so with a sense of purpose and a deep understanding of the significance of my presence. I am no longer confined by the judgements of others or the limiting beliefs that once held me back. Instead, I stand tall, empowered by the knowledge that my journey of self-discovery and breaking barriers has not only transformed my life but has also contributed to a more inclusive and equitable world for all.

Having experienced firsthand the challenges as an immigrant, I am now determined to help others like me find their true selves and reach their full potential. I have become actively involved in mentoring and guiding first- and second-generation immigrant women, sharing my own struggles and triumphs to inspire them on their journeys. Whether it's offering guidance on life's decisions, navigating the personal growth process or simply being a compassionate listener, I strive to be a beacon of support for those who face similar obstacles.

In this pursuit, I firmly believe that when we lift others up, we collectively elevate society as a whole. Through my actions, I hope to create a ripple effect that fosters a more understanding and accepting world, where all individuals are encouraged to embrace their unique qualities and passions. By helping others find their true selves and empowering them to overcome barriers, I aim to contribute to a society that not only values diversity but celebrates it as a powerful force for positive change.

CATAREEYA MARSDEN

Mindset coach for 1st & 2nd Generation Immigrant Women

Connect: catmarsden.com / @hellocatmarsden

KATE NEILSON
BEYOND THE SURFACE: THE HIDDEN STRUGGLES OF LOVE & ADDICTION

I have been to many dark places, many times in my life, but somehow, some way I always seem to go into survival mode and pull myself away from the toxicity of who and how I got there in the first place. Learning to recognise what's not good for me and what's no longer serving me anymore. This is now my key to happiness … being able to know my worth and know I AM ENOUGH. I am imperfectly perfect.

Life throws us great challenges sometimes; I can certainly relate to this on so many levels. Coming from a family where I was an only child, I didn't have siblings I could go to when something went wrong in my life. I was always a fighter and I've overcome the toughest of relationships, but I never gave up.

I lost my father tragically when I was thirty years old, and I remember it being the most painful memory I have ever had to endure in my life. My one and only male figure that had been there to always genuinely love and take care of me was gone. Suddenly. No goodbyes. No final hug. No I love you. Just gone. I had no siblings to lean on, just my Mum and me. The tears that came for months were endless. The pain of not having a father figure in my life ever again was torture. I will grieve forever … I will never get over the loss, but instead learn to live with it. As long as I am living, I'll carry him with me. But one thing I did learn is to be grateful every second of every day that you get to spend with people you love. Life is so very precious.

Being in the spotlight for so many years and being in a relationship with someone that also had a profile in Australia is always going to be scrutinised and have its pros and cons.

An AFL footballer and a model was for sure a great headliner for the media, one that I endured for years to come.

I was one of the faces of the F1 Grand Prix, being amongst one of the first Grid Girls to inspire a trend that would later go down in the history books as an iconic part of the 2000s. Rubbing shoulders with the likes of Michael Schumacher and David Coulthard, sipping drinks with Priscilla Presley and staying up late at parties to enjoy the high I was on. Either from the cocaine I was regularly snorting or just the high of getting a taste of the limelight.

But with every high there is usually always a low.

I fell in love with someone I thought I would spend the rest of my life with, someone who later proposed to me in front of my whole family. Someone who was more in the media than I ever was, someone I travelled the world with, but someone who was also known for being in scandals – scandals involving women. Something that would later traumatise me for a very long time. From a whirlwind romance that quickly turned into love, the highs were so high I never wanted to come out of the clouds. Insatiable in every way, to a point you would breathe and intoxicate yourself from this thing called love. Living together and making every moment count. But as they say, what goes up must eventually come down, and when your highs are extreme then expect the lows to be extremely low.

My lows were unfortunately very publicised, but I chose that life and so what didn't kill me ultimately made me stronger. I just remember headline after headline putting pressure on me to question why I am even in this relationship to begin with? Why keep putting myself through the pain of someone not respecting my boundaries and who emotionally almost destroyed me and couldn't tell the truth even when faced with it head-on?

The holidays that turned into arrests and trashed hotel rooms. Drug-fuelled benders that turned into depression. Sleepless nights worrying about when the next blow-up would be and the uncertainty of not knowing when he was going to come home or if he even was coming home. The vicious cycle of infidelity which plagued his life before, during and after me. The pain being so great you would feel like jumping off our penthouse balcony. So many obstacles that it felt almost impossible to overcome. I felt at one point totally emotionally defeated.

I'm sure this book is not long enough for me to explain the exact nature and details of what was to come and what I endured for all those years, but I know the roller-coaster we call 'love' is one hell of a ride.

If anyone knows the cycle of addiction it's me … knowing something or someone is bad for you but unable to break the pattern of being able to leave or get out of the toxicity I was living through. Living off the extreme highs, knowing the lows were far worse than you ever imagined.

Turning to drugs to socialise and numb the pain, only to realise you yourself are becoming an addict.

But I eventually healed and I also learnt how to forgive. I didn't want to carry the burden of pain any longer so I had to let it go.

It would be many years later that I met someone who became what I thought was my soulmate, my forever, but who threw me straight back into the cycle of dishonesty and betrayal. A cycle I was well familiarised with. How could this be happening? I am a solid, loyal and compassionate soul that loves with every ounce of her being and loves with her whole entire heart. My poor body. My poor mind. Knowing that the one person you really truly love, someone you would lay your life on the line for could deceive you so effortlessly. The feelings of stress and anxiety, the tears and the constant never-ending pain that come with the never ending WHYs? Being suddenly triggered by past traumas and having a partner that is ignorant to your pain. I just wanted to say to him, 'Never ignore a person who loves you, cares for you and misses you. Because one day, you might wake up from your sleep and realise that you lost the moon while counting the stars.'

Then when you finally wake up one day from the depths of that despair, when things can't get any worse and you say to yourself:

What change am I going to make or cause?

That's the question we get to wake up to every day. Who must I become to create a complete change? And I'm not going to do it all in one day, I'm not going to do it all in one week, not even a month. It might take me a year, but I'm willing to spend my life becoming and creating and causing the complete change that I'm responsible for. We need to give ourselves permission to be on the inside of the frame. I don't want to look at the picture, I want to help draw it. I want to use my divine colours. My colours aren't your colours and my lines aren't your lines and my journey is not your journey, but I've got some colour to add, I've got some lines to draw and I've got some contribution to bring and I'm not going to do it all perfect but my imperfections might just have some progress in it.

I saw myself in the mirror. I saw all my imperfections, I saw all my drama, I saw this white skin and full lips and brown hair, my skinny body that wasn't celebrated as being beautiful. I saw it all, I blamed it all. I saw the girl in In the mirror from Tasmania who ended up in the ICU, I saw the girl who eventually ended up in rehab, I saw the girl that lost her father so tragically, I saw the girl who was traumatised by her past relationships, I saw the girl that fought so hard for someone she loved and got nowhere, I saw all my imperfections before I saw my greatness.

I saw all the reasons why I shouldn't stand up and I shouldn't get up and I shouldn't speak up for what I believe in. Who am I? Look at my history. And then I suddenly realised … look at ME … and look at my history … and oh with a past like that I'm perfect for a time like this.

It's not in spite of your story you get to do great things and be a revolutionary of change … it's BECAUSE of your story that you ARE the change and you ARE the revolution, you ARE the conversation, you ARE the evidence. If you want some evidence, look to your left and your right and tell them you ARE the evidence. You're the evidence that all great things still come through. You're the evidence that we get to rise a thousand times. You are the evidence that love does prevail. You are the evidence that God and the Universe are gods of a thousand second chances. Hell, if anyone knows this it's me. I always tell myself now, *You're a fighter. Look at everything you have overcome. Don't give up now … your life has just begun.*

I'm not saying I'm perfect … what I have learned how to do is perfectly be with my imperfections. I've learned how to embrace my journey.

I talked about that mirror, and I came to the mirror with so much stress and anxiety and self-doubt. I didn't even realise how I got there. Do you ever get somewhere and you're like, 'How did I get here? Hey, what happened? What left turn did I make when I was supposed to go right?' Somewhere along the way I lost Kate, somewhere along the line I was a great server of others, I was a great lover of others, I was a great lifter-upper of others and I mastered that. Somehow, I began to love and lift everyone up higher than me, and I ended up somewhere that I didn't see coming. And when I looked in the mirror I had to remind myself you ARE enough, you ARE beautiful, you ARE strong and you ARE worthy. Oh, I have to cut the shackles to blame, shame, guilt, regret and anger every day, and every day they tried to tether themselves back to me again and every day I had to cut them again. No, no, no … I forgave myself for you yesterday. See, self-love is not a one and done, you don't arrive when you love yourself because you don't even know what's around the corner next month. So, you have to choose to love yourself again. The more you know the more you have got to keep choosing to love yourself.

Who are you becoming? When you give yourself permission to show up and shine, unapologetically, and when you realise that you don't get to be amazing in spite of your past ... but it's BECAUSE of your past that you're perfect for such a time. Who better can rock us through this time than you? I learnt to be intentional about it, unapologetic about it, non-negotiable about it. I stopped taking score on who might approve of me shining brightly. I came here so bright, it would take me more effort to keep dimming my light than it would to just let it go. And I realised the world will be a better place with all my imperfections in it. DO YOU, because no-one can do you. If you can be anyone in this world ... be you. Don't worry about what other people think ... it's just a thought and that's why you can't see it.

The trauma of my past has not only made me grateful for all the good times but more importantly all the bad. I now, after a long and tedious journey, know my self-worth. And no-one will ever take that from me again. I have risen up and seen the light and oh how clearly I now see. My mistakes of tolerating bad behaviour for so long are no longer a part of my future. I now stand up for who I am and what I believe in and the only way to accomplish my dreams and goals is to move forward and up. Nothing or no-one is going to stop me from achieving the life I have always wanted. You are either by my side equally or you're out. My vibration is high and nothing or no-one is going to lower it ever again. When love is real and genuine, it doesn't lie, cheat, pretend, hurt you or make you feel unwanted. It's supposed to be a cure to all your worries. Imagine being with someone who makes you believe in love again. Someone who treats you right this time and cares about you as much as you care about them. Be with someone who will take care of you, not materialistically, but takes care of your soul, your wellbeing, your heart and everything that is you.

Self-love is not a sprint but it's a marathon ...

My faith in God and my faith in the Universe is what has got me to where I am today. It's taught me to believe. Believe in yourself.

The rarest of all human qualities is consistency … so consistently show up for yourself … because YOU are all you have got.

I've lost people that are closest to me and tragically … over and over … to suicide, through car accidents, through illness … so I've always said:

Enjoy the ride. Tomorrow is never promised … so f#%*ng live your life today! This thing that we call life is a gift … time is a gift … something we have one shot at. When my ex-boyfriend took his own life with the world at his feet and the stunning good looks he attained from birth, I was shattered, but it made me realise we need to create hope and fight the fight.

It doesn't matter how slow you go … as long as you don't stop the fight. Because sometimes darkness finds cracks within the light and wins. I want to help stop that. Stop the darkness from defeating the light. And we will win … together.

In the face of adversity, I've navigated through dark places, finding strength to detach from toxicity and recognise my own worth. Life's challenges, from family dynamics to high-profile relationships, have taught me resilience. Amidst highs and lows, I've grappled with addiction cycles, but I've also encountered moments of love and betrayal. The realisation that change starts with me drives me forward. Embracing imperfections, my past shapes me as an agent of transformation. I'm a testament that even in the midst of struggle, positive change is possible. The trajectory of my life has led me to embrace self-worth and self-love, fortified by faith. Amidst losses, I've learned to seize each day and battle darkness with hope. My journey is a marathon, one where consistency and self-fighting matter. Together, we can overcome and prevent the encroachment of darkness, embodying the victorious power of light. Amen.

KATE NEILSON

Actress / Producer / Host
Connect: @kateneilsonofficial

DAVID THACKER
A WALK OF FAITH, SAVING GRACE & A REDEMPTIVE PLACE

In my late teens, I was great at sport and that was my thing – I was Dave the fitness guy, Dave the athlete, Dave the runner. I knew that when I left school, I wanted to become a personal trainer – it just made sense to me. I pursed this career and did all things health and fitness, early mornings, late nights, not a problem, I loved my job.

During this time, I use to box through my local boxing gym. I boxed for three years straight, but then while training for a professional fight I got injured. I'd severely damaged my neck and I had to stop. Two weeks after this, an extras/acting agency were looking for a boxer, I joined the agency and was sent to the audition, I was called the next day ... you've got the job! I was then featured in a high-profile feature film getting direction from one of the best in the business. One door had closed but another had opened.

This ignited my passion for both health and fitness and acting in both film and television. I did many extras, featured extras, fifty-worders, body double and TVCs. This was great for a while, but I wanted a greater challenge, so I decided as mature-aged student in my mid-twenties to get a degree in health (PDHPE) to become a health teacher.

Before finishing my degree I did volunteer work in Ethiopia, visiting hospitals and communities and having great talks with great leaders about what needed to happen to make things work better in communities and in the country. This sparked a passion and desire for community development and creating a difference in the world through my skill set.

Arriving back in Australia and then finishing my degree, I pursed work in Australian Indigenous communities where I worked for five years in different settings, working as community developer helping people connect with services and events and contributing to the overall function of the community. These types of jobs are based in remote areas of Australia and are often isolated. This is a rich culture with beautiful people and ancient wisdom to passed on and passed down – I cherished my time doing this work.

After five years, I finished this line of work and decided to work offshore (overseas) in a FIFO role (fly-in, fly-out) position. This would consist of three flights then put your bags down and go to work, this would be the start of either a two on two off weeks or three on three off weeks, and shifts would often be twelve hours a day for two to three weeks straight.

The work I was involved in was looking after people seeking asylum and hoping for refugee status. Within three rotations of working, a riot broke out and a man had been murdered. Weeks after this event I saw a man hang himself, but luckily he was rescued with moments to spare with a pocket knife that the security guards have with a special device to cut rope quickly.

In these environments what's right seems wrong and what is wrong is made out to be right.s As a person with a strong belief system, this troubled me; I didn't understand how to be or what to do. If you showed too much compassion it was a bad thing, if you did too much for someone it was a bad thing. Following process and procedure was the name of the game, you were told this is a hard job but you are getting paid a lot of money for it, if it's not for you leave and someone will readily take your place.

As a person who couldn't switch off and just do, I considered my options. This was the sliding door moment, I was convinced at this point that doing a job for a not-for-profit company that was also working in the same environment was the better choice. So I waited until I had a rotation off and politely informed my company that I would no longer be working for them but thank you for experience. The moment I sent this email, it was instant regret. What had I just done? Yes, the work was hard but I was earning great money.

Then I transferred to my new job, same role different overseas location ... I got there and thought, *What have I done?* The new job was not only harder but the working environment was toxic, again what seemed wrong was right what was right seemed wrong. I remember being dropped off at a location on the island by myself with ten clients, no car to leave, no communication devices, I was told, 'Dave, these guys might pour petrol on themselves and try and kill themself make sure they don't.'

I thought up until this point I was okay with dealing with problems, I'd lived in remote Australian communities, I'm pretty resilient ... wrong. The nature of the work and the toxic work environment had taken its toll, within ten days of being there I had lost 15kg of body weight. My brain was in overdrive. *What is going on?* My brain had shut down and my fight-or-flight response had kicked in.

Again, I waited until I got time off and politely informed them after a few rotations I would not be coming back.

Time for a holiday. I toured Australia and thought this will be how I will cure my woes. I jumped off cliffs and went shark cage diving to try and bring enjoyment back into my life, I went on retreats, I read good books, I exercised, I thought I was okay ...

I realised down the line, though, my reality had changed, *Why do I feel different? I'm the same person but with different feelings, why am I interrupting the world this way, I never use to be like this ... what's going on??*

I tried to figure out what was happening by myself but nothing really hit the mark. I saw a doctor and he told me I was experiencing PTSD. I told him I felt extremely wound up inside at the same time as being extremely tired, I felt like someone had wound my brain up with a key and I couldn't switch it off.

I lived with this feeling in me day in and day out, *Why was I so sensitive to certain environments? Why do noises effect me in ways they never use to before? Why am I reacting this way?*

For three years I experienced this reality on a daily basis. As time went by my coping mechanisms started to change, I no longer exercised to deal with my stress, I started to use alcohol to dull pain, I convinced myself its okay, it's organic preservative-free red wine, it's good for you, good for your heart, good for your health. I was never addicted to alcohol, but I did use it as a coping mechanism, which I thought was helping me deal with the problem but it was actually making it worse. The effect on my brain and my body was not great, I was consuming alcohol whilst being on medication, the amount I was having was never the problem, the fact that it was now my go-to was.

After subjecting my body and my mind to this reactive response on and off for three years I'd put on 10-15kg of weight.

As the weight gain was gradual, I didn't really notice it until the three-year mark. I then saw a doctor who asked for me to get a blood test, and the results came back that I was pre-diabetic. As I didn't have a family history of it I asked how I had got this way. He told me it was my lifestyle, I needed to lose weight and get will re-tested in six months.

At this moment I realised my mortality, so I felt the need to change my mentality. I started training again, eating better and stopped drinking alcohol immediately. Six months passed and I was back for another blood test where I was informed I was now type two diabetic ... what?

I said I've being doing all the right things and now I was worse? I asked what could happen if you don't look after diabetes. Well, he replied, you can lose your eyesight, get liver or kidney damage and we may have to amputate your toes and/or your feet.

I told them I had tried to lose weight and asked what else I could do. I was offered a weight-loss medication. I was given three to chose from, so I chose one and was informed it had incremental dosages – one a day for the first week, two a day for the second week and so on.

I started taking the medication the first week, one a day; I felt okay but had a little bit of a strange feeling like I was on a boat. I got to the second week and started to take two tablets, and *boom* ... drug-induced psychosis. It was as if a hurricane had gone through my brain, my mind was infiltrated with hallucinations, I had a duality of knowing I was crazy but at the same time thinking what I was thinking was real. That is the scariest thing I have ever experienced. I drove myself to the hospital thinking I would be treated and sent home, but I was placed in a patient transport vehicle and put in a psychiatric hospital for five days, wearing the same clothes as I was on arrival.

What you experience in a physchosis is a reality of the world that is now tainted, you have the feeling like people are out to get you for no reason. As a health teacher, I have lots of sports equipment at home, I remember I got a baseball bat out and placed it beside my bed, thinking if they're coming at least I'll be ready for them. I don't know what schizophrenia is like but I imagine it may feel something like that did. I was afraid to say what I was thinking because it was crazy to me and I was scared of being judged. People thinking you're crazy whilst you're crazy doesn't help, so I kept it to myself. I remember people looking at me though and asking me, 'What's happened? The brightness in your eyes has gone away.' I would tell them I was unwell, there is an expression they use in Italian which means 'not quite right', you are here but not there – this is how I felt, not quite right. My only real saving grace at this point were the friendly chats with baristas in the morning, that's all I could really do, I'd focus myself enough to do just that, to get a coffee and go home ... agoraphobia had set in.

The effects of the psychosis continued for six months. At the end of the six-month mark one night I'd considered taking my life. I'd never thought this before, never wanted to do something like this before, it was just a dark night, the darkest of nights, I had a fishing knife in my equipment, I wrote my will and that night was going to be the night.

I put the blade to my chest and tried to force it into my body. I was unsuccessful, but I did however have a wound in my chest that needed hospital attention. I drove myself to the hospital with blood on my shirt and asked to see a doctor. They put me a on hospital bed and put things on my fingers and other things on my chest and a specialist came in to give me a ultrasound. They told me that depending on how deep it was they might need to operate. I asked what that would involve and they said they cut your chest open and try and put things back together. Luckily the wound was just superficial and nothing needed to be done, but this was a wake-up call.

I was then placed on another medication to help me get over the weight-loss medication. This medication makes you put on weight, and within three months I'd become 13kg heavier.

I paid a visit to an endocrinologist, and they informed me my blood sugar was through the roof, if I didn't do something about it I would be insulin dependent and be on injections every morning as if I now had type one diabetes.

I went home determined this wouldn't not happen, I had to do things the good old-fashioned way. I got on the internet, found the best pair of shoes I could buy and bought a gym membership at my local gym. I thought back to when my mind had the most strength, the most clarity and I was reminded of bible verse John 8:32, 'And you will know the truth, and the truth will set you free.'

I bought a series of books from the same author, these were the books in my past that had meant the most to me. The first book I read was the discipline of grace, depicting a disciplined dependency on God, I do the work God does the growth; this was the start of my health and fitness journey.

To give context and time frame, my journey started just before COVID-19. A global pandemic was an interesting time to try and recover from psychosis – thinking you're crazy and trying to understand your place in the world whilst the world was crazy itself was a hard thing to do. The small amount supportive friends and family I had around me and God's grace and monkey grip he had on my life saved me. I feel in life you don't necessarily need many friends but the ones you have are snipers; what I mean by this is that they hit the mark, they get you, they are there for you and if they don't understand they listen.

I wanted to know my Lord and Saviour again, who was He? What was He? How was He? What was my life like before all of this happened? What does Good look like? Do I try and make things as they were before or is this a new path, did I just go through a refining process of hardship to create something different ... to create someone different ?

Time to do the work. I start with my mornings with prayer. 'Search me, O God, and know my heart; test me and know my anxious thoughts. See if the is and grievous way in me and lead me in the way everlasting.' – Psalms 139:23-24.

My journey back to health and happiness was a slow one. I reflected on my time years before where I sought pleasure to cure my hardship and realised this isn't the solution, and doing the same thing over and over and expecting a different result is itself insanity. I now seek peace, to be still, to surrender to what I know is good, right and just. I feel as though I'm still in the wilderness but I have a compass.

The days and weeks started slow and inconsistent , I knew what I should be doing but what I felt like doing it wasn't there yet. I changed my goal, instead of trying to achieve big targets, I tried to achieve small targets but consistently – instead of doing thirty to sixty minutes of exercise a day I do twenty. I started with three times a week, then worked my way up to five. During that process I wasn't focusing on diet, just on getting myself moving again, as I trained my body, I trained my mind, and I gradually gave myself the capability and competency to make better and stronger choices.

At the three-month mark I focused on diet, started eating whole foods instead of processed food, I educated myself on what I eat, how I eat and why I eat. This was my process for another three months but now increasing my exercise to five times a week thirty minutes a day.

I came to the realisation at this point that you can listen to books via audio, so I no longer did my exercise and then read my books, I now had it in my ears as I trained. Through acting and teaching I've learnt that I'm a kinaesthetic learner – the act of doing something whilst learning something opens up a whole new world.

I was now in the zone I like to refer to as Forrest Gumping it, 'I just kept on running.' Things were no longer a mental exercise, rather a physical exercise that was helping me in all aspects of my life.

The next three months I learnt about fasting, intermittent fasting, to be precise, I learn about eating in windows of time but using the time around that window effectively, the clarity of mind, my connection to God, my understanding of myself became more vivid.

The aim at this point was restoring health and fitness, but weight loss followed suit the kilos were falling off and my confidence slowly restored.

The next three months were a building phrase, increasing the resistance training, enduring the discomfort, as discomfort equals growth.

Somewhere along this time line I was introduced to ice baths and cold immersion therapy, breathwork and mediation, mindfulness, infrared saunas, you name it ...

I now have a tool belt of activities to get involved with, communities to be part of, also finding a place of worship for me in a spirit-filled environment that understands God's capacity to heal, God's capacity to restore hope, to put back together what has been pulled apart. *Anakefaliaieao,* the Greek word meaning to gather up and put back together – this is what I needed to live in grace and truth and act in the metanoia meaning to change one's mind; to expend it in such a way to have a new perspective of the world and oneself.

A year and a half later, I'm 26kg lighter and still going. As I reflect on it maybe my journey didn't start a year and a half ago, maybe it started ten years when I decided to leave my job and go to another. Maybe things start at birth and we are all here to learn, grow and understand ourselves better, the people around us and the world we live in. For me it's now about the creator that brought me here and allowed me to experience this amazing thing called life.

Where to from here? What does this next chapter look like, I always try and ask myself, what does good look like, if I had a canvas, what does it look like what would I paint ? Why would I paint it?

I feel like

I'm in a good place, I've come to understand that with things like neuroplasticity creating new biological pathways in the brain you override things and when you take the emotional charge out of a situation it gets stored in the soul as wisdom.

So I hope I can give insight, help and an understanding to those out there reading this, that there is a God, He is your friend, He will help you, you can do it ...

DAVID THACKER
Personal Trainer
Connect: @hotpropty

KAREN WEAVER
A POSITIVE FROM A NEGATIVE

T here'll be many times in your life where you will endure some tough times, that is life. The big difference in the result is how we react and what our emotional and mental capacity is at the time.

I know this from experience. I have endured rock bottom in my life, it was because of something that would have generally just shaken off and got on with life but because my cup was empty during that period of my life it was the last straw that broke me and I fell into PTSD.

We will all endure different levels of severities, of tough times, but we'll also all be at different strengths, the mind at different times. It's often when we're at our lowest when things go wrong, because whenever we're hanging out at a high vibration, everything seems to flow well. I studied a lot of that and went into lots of psychology and also metaphysics, and I've studied all of that. But I want to share with you two things in two points in my life where I feel benefit readers because I've come through them, so that you may have a different perspective about them that may be helpful.

The first time was back in 2007. I was always someone who was positive, who always was there for others, who was a bright, shining light when I walked into a room. Didn't really care too much about what people thought, I just got on with life and my journey. I never really knew what I wanted to do in life but I honoured the journey and loved my zest for life, so not having a purpose didn't bother me because in hindsight I knew I was doing groundwork. My drive and curiosity and all of those wonderful things that keep you feeling alive and energised, I had bucket loads of that!

In 2006, I had my second son. I chose to breastfeed him and it was tough going! Breastfeeding in Ireland was only just becoming something that was encouraged after decades of a formula culture. I was tired and giving my all to motherhood and my family. So a few months later when an incident happened in my home it just knocked the stuffing out of me. It sunk me and I fell into PTSD. I remember the exact moment when it was like an out of body experience, where I was standing right next to myself, looking at myself. I was tired and in despair at what had just happened but the biggest and most overwhelming feeling was to know that nothing would ever be the same again. Everything I was working hard to maintain and juggle could never be the same and it was such a shock to my nervous system that I went into survival mode in the form of PTSD.

I knew in that moment that everything from that point would be different, it would never be the same again. I felt out of control and unsafe, unsteady and numb! For someone so vibrant to become a shell of themselves who had tunnel vision, I literally couldn't see peripherally it wasn't a good time in my life because how are you support to attract wonderful things when you are numb emotionally.

But there was one blessing that got me through and that was knowledge! I had previously worked in a mental health environment for 4 years before having my second child. This equip me with the knowledge to understand what was happening to me, I didn't like it, but I didn't fear it and I knew what I needed to do to come through it. So instead of it being an unproductive time in my life I can reflect back now and know that I did so much inner work, work that stands to me to this day.

I am reluctant to say that it was a blessing, but I can honestly hand on heart say that I wouldn't be who I am today if I hadn't of gone through it. I definitely believe that I would never have made the decision to emigrate to Australia and that was a great decision for me.

I think that's a huge thing with PTSD is that you're having flashbacks when you go to think or go there with your thoughts or speak about it, you start to shake all of those things, so you just kind of become quiet. I had tunnel vision for a long time, whereas I could only see in front of me, and there was no peripheral vision, so even physically, things were not good. I would just take it easy and go one day at a time, do what I could, and not put pressure on me. My focus would be on my boys and day to day. I went totally inwards and in reflection I call it my cocoon period. I was inwards doing the work because I was giving so much of myself and not taking time to get to know me and what makes me tick. Yes, I had done lots of that work in my childhood because I was curious. I was allowed the grace of finding who I was. I just loved life. It loved me back but I my soul had never struggled, I never knew the depths of grief or despair but I did now and I was going to learn more about these depths when the next incident happened.

So there I was in my cocoon period, doing all of the inner work, and then a wakeup call happened in the form of a double miscarriage, and that broke my heart.

We were at 12 weeks when I lost one, and we went to the hospital for confirmation of the loss, I was a wreck, I couldn't stop crying. When we went into the room they did a scan and to my absolute joy and confusion there was a heartbeat! In that moment I had an overwhelming feeling of hope and joy mixed with sadness for the loss also.

For the next 2 weeks I lay in total bedrest praying for it to be saved, I knew my younger sister was a twin and my mother took to the bed and she was saved, surely mine would be saved too. I prayed to my granny in heaven to please help let this baby survive. But all of my prayers didn't stop the loss that happened in one moment when I felt a pop and gush and that was it, my baby was gone. It was just so heartbreaking and see-ing it on the screen meant I was so connected. It broke my heart to lose the twin and I remember lying at night, praying to God to please let me be full again, that I just felt so empty. Even though I had two children, I just couldn't understand, why me? Why was this happening to me when I had birthed two healthy boys? Why did I lose these twins?

Midwives told me to get on with life, that miscarriages happen all of the time and its normal. But it wasn't 'normal' for me I had to grieve and I honoured that grief. I am a great believer that grief is different for us all, there is no one size fits all so we have to do what works for us no matter what others say.

For me, I had this unsatiable need to understand, why me? Why then?

And it wasn't until two and a half years later when I had actually emigrated to Australia with my family and had my fourth child and life was so different that a realisation came! I was watching The View and one of the hosts, Whoopi Goldberg, said something that was like a total lightning bolt epiphany moment for me.

It went like this… A reality tv couple came on the show and they had recently endured a miscarriage and it was brought up, the woman was evidently still grieving and Whoopi turned her back to the camera and said something along the lines of *'I am going to tell you something that I tell all of my friends who endure this loss, this was a Visitor that came to help you back onto the right path on life and when you shift onto the right path your gift will come.'*

It was in that moment I realised that the miscarriage was a visitor that came to help me get back on the right track in life and when I made that choice and that decision to get back on the right track in life, everything started to flow again.

And I realised that's what happened to me, because when I had my double miscarriage, it knocked me out of my PTSD and I started to feel again, because when you have PTSD, you're numb to emotion, you don't feel things and how are you supposed to attract wonderful things into your life when you are emotionless. It's just a really profound experience.

When the PTSD happened to me, I was numb to life. And then when I woke up from it, everything started to flow right because beforehand cars would break down, money wasn't coming, we were in difficulty, lots of horrible things would happen. And then when I woke up to life again and started to feel again and started to get enthused by life, everything started to go right. Even though my initial feels were of sadness and despair, they were emotions I could work through. The line was so definitive and I started to have a bright outlook and everything. We got our visas to go to Australia, we got married, and the most magical thing was that I got pregnant straight away and waddled my way 35 weeks pregnant to Australia, everything worked out.

And I realised in that moment from what Whoopi said that I had received a Visitor and I took the action needed to get out of PTSD and get back on the right track.

I felt absolutely compelled to share this discovery with other and so I wrote a blog post, that wasn't enough so when the energetic call to do NaNoWrimo, which is National Novel Writing Month, and I started to write a novel. Why a novel? I don't know, I just knew it was a call I couldn't ignore so I honoured it and I showed up and wrote 1667 words a day for 30 days and I had a 50000 word novel on Dec1, 2010. I don't know how this novel came out of me, I was terrible at English at school, I really want to emphasise that because I didn't let that block me, I just honoured the process without any expectation of results. I wrote the book in service to help others who may walk a similar path.

The Visitor: a magical understanding of uncertainty was born then and it was a catalyst into all of the wonderful I now experience today, it's actually being picked up to be made into a tv series, which is really cool. And it shows you that when you show up and when you identify, when you honour the journey, the good and the bad, you will be rewarded, amazing things can happen. But you have got to show up. You've got to go through the adversities and learn the lessons in them. Yes, I got stuck in PTSD for 14 months, but I came out of it. I wasn't defined by it for a lifetime. And I learned the lessons that I needed to in that time and I emerged from the cocoon.

I now understand the importance of taking care of me first, because when I give the best to myself I am then able to give the best of myself to others and when adversities happen in life, which they do for us all, then I don't fall below the line, instead I stumble, steady myself for a moment and get back to the journey. I know the power of the pause and that allenges are often here to help us grow into the next version of ourselves so that our dreams and goals are the very next step. You can't avoid the development work, you have to learn as you go, feel ok with discomfort when it is around and know that it is there to service your growth.

It is my hope that my story help you see the potential in pain, to honour it but not let it define your lifetime, carry it but don't let it weigh you down, learn from it and grow into a higher version of yourself, one that your future self will thank you for. And most importantly it doesn't have to be perfect!

KAREN WEAVER

Publisher / Mentor / Multi-Genre Author & Speaker
Connect:kmdbooks.com/@karenmcdermottpublisher

CLAIRE SMITH
FROM UNWORTHY TO WORTHY: THE STRENGTH OF BEING DIFFERENT

I t's funny how you can look back at your life and see defining moments, in which a simple comment or conversation can have such a profound impact on your life and journey. I must have been around fourteen years old at school when this happened to me, stood with the cool girls desperately trying to fit in but never feeling like I did. At that age all you ever want is to fit in somewhere and be accepted. Listening to a conversation that went like this: 'If I was seeing a boy and he hit me but was good-looking that would be fine because he's good-looking.' From that conversation I instantly felt in my body a rush of panic, fear and unworthiness – it was like a punch in the gut. I saw myself as not fitting in, a bit awkward, shy and ugly. I never smoked but stood with the girls who did; I never got the rude jokes but laughed along.

Let me explain how such an indirect and silly comment would affect me or take me to such an extreme/visceral feeling about myself as that teenager. Growing up in a small village in the city of Durham, UK. Having two older brothers, I was always a tomboy, loving to play sports, especially football. Prior to high school, life was so much easier. Younger kids just accept things so much easier. Playing games, being a tomboy was easy for me because I was naturally good at football, the boys never treated me any differently. However, my teenage years were hard, the boys saw me as one of them and because of that I felt like they would never ask me out and with the girls I just felt withdrawn and not myself, I always felt different. I didn't wear make-up, my mum wouldn't let me dye my hair – which is a blessing now as I've still never dyed it, she would say, 'When you're older you'll be sick of dying it.' I felt very confused being attracted to girls and not boys but not knowing why.

That statement made me react in such a way because, in my eyes, who would ever love me? If no boy would ask me out and I was ugly, I had no chance of a relationship. My first interest in girls was probably in my first year of high school, I had a crush on the maths teacher. I had no idea what the feelings and emotions were, and of course the hormones are very strong at that age. I never had crushes on boys but would pretend to like famous people, more so footballers but for the football. You would cover your bedroom wall with posters from magazines like *Smash Hits*, with your favourite pop stars, band or movie star. I would myself have posters for some years to come of Madonna all over. I remember my great-auntie, whom I had a very special relationship with but was a very conservative lady, thought Madonna was just outrageous for the times, in the eighties especially her biggest hit 'Like a Virgin' I would sing it with no idea what the song was about.

Trying to grapple with my feelings, I would cry myself to sleep praying to God that I would wake up in the morning and be normal and not have these feelings. Asking myself, *What is wrong with me?* For sure I did not know anyone who was different like I was, and from what I heard from school and society it was very bad. I felt so ashamed of hiding such a terrible secret. I would have done anything to be 'normal' like all the other girls. I would never ever have voiced how I felt and didn't really trust anyone in my circle to confide in. I would physically throw up in the toilets most days from anxiety. Trying to fit in was a constant battle for me. I remember going out to a pub around the time we were leaving school, I just felt so uncomfortable, guys coming on to us, trying to chat our group up. I just wanted the ground to swallow me up, I felt so awkward in my own skin.

My people-pleasing started in my late teens, feeling like I needed to buy friendship because me as myself just wasn't enough. During my college years I would restrict my food; I felt like that was something I had total control over and maybe being thin would make me more accepted. Going back to the times of the eighties and nineties, the views of people were so different there was no diversity, inclusivity or awareness. There was no internet, mobile phones, social media or Google, even the word *gay* if I did hear it, I only thought about men, I had no idea that included women. The world back then nobody spoke about mental health issues or needed support from professional experts. You just shut up and put up. No-one wanted to talk about anything taboo. People just didn't know anything different back then.

I joined Newcastle women's football team when I was around eighteen years old. I wasn't allowed to play for the school as only boys could play, back in those days girls weren't allowed to wear trousers for school. Finding a football team was amazing. Some of the girls were openly out at football. It was a whole new world for me, I had never met anyone else who was attracted to the same sex and certainly not a group where everyone involved was so okay with it. It was like our little bubble. From about the age of twenty-one I would go out to bars and nightclubs. Great times, I found a place where I felt I belonged, but still I never had confidence in myself to ask girls out with this debilitating fear of rejection through not feeling good enough. Always thinking back to that teenager who wasn't, in my eyes, pretty. I based everything on looks back then and mainly my lack of beauty. I failed to see the true essence of a person, from the inside out, which is what really matters.

My own coming out story is quite comical, looking back. I was around twenty-two years old and my mum and I were on spa weekend. I had recently had my first tattoo done so I knew she would see it. I sat my mum down and said, 'Mum, I've got something very important to tell you and I really hope you are not disappointed in me.' She stopped me in my tracks and said, 'Claire, I know what it is, me and your dad have always known, we love you exactly as you are, all we want is for you to be happy.' I said, 'I was going to say I have a tattoo, but that's amazing.' We hugged and laughed at the misunderstanding. I cried, for me it was pure relief for getting such a secret off my chest and knowing everything was okay. In my mind, I had created a whole scenario where I might be abandoned, unloved or rejected by the people I loved the most in the world. Looking back on this coming out story, I don't think I ever said the words, but I didn't have to. I know my parents love me unconditionally. I know my mum was concerned about how the outside world would see me or accept me and purely from a perspective that she didn't want me to experience pain or be upset by comments or anything like that. She and my dad have always supported me; my mum would come to pick out an engagement ring for my future partner in years to come. Always very accepting of my girlfriends and enjoying spending time with them. That always made me feel seen and valued.

I feel very fortunate at my coming out story. I had a friend once who didn't have such a good response. I can't speak specifically about how it made him feel but I know it must have been hard, his family did not react well. However, his boyfriend's family took him in as his own and eventually his family did come round. Sometimes people just need time to come to terms with it, and I promise anyone in this situation, there will always be someone who will support and love you through such a time. We must not forget it is still illegal in over sixty countries in the world. I can't imagine having to keep a secret or enter a relationship that is not your preferred choice for fear of being put into prison. I have good memories from going to London pride in 2000 and 2001 and being part of the pride march and the energy and comradery to raise our flags and be part of a huge community. I will never forget being with my friends and listening to 'The Power of Love' by Frankie goes to Hollywood in Hyde Park and the love and support of everybody there.

Although my family have been nothing but supportive, the thing about coming out is it's a constant thing in your life. For some reason it can feel more uncomfortable with strangers or acquaintances who don't know the real you. In the past this has been a real obstacle for me, when asked are you married, do you have kids and the like. Weighing up will this person be okay if I speak my truth or is it better to say nothing for fear of being judged, rejected or shamed.

My deep-rooted sense of feeling unworthy in my own skin would hold me back from opportunities for most of my life and this continued limiting belief that I wasn't enough as I am. A belief is a thought you think over and over and, in my case, a belief which did not serve me but would manifest itself into real-life situations to continue to hold me back. In my career as a group fitness instructor, I didn't take opportunities earlier for fear of being judged or told I wasn't good enough, but if you don't put yourself out there you will never get the experience or opportunities for what I now see as feedback, to grow and become better at what you do.

The biggest issues around how I saw myself would be in romantic relationships; I would pick emotionally unavailable (avoidant) people. When the relationship would end, I would point to myself and say, *Well, it's your fault you are not deserving of love, or good enough*, and blame myself for the breakdown. Reinforcing that belief I had. I never felt I deserved a fully loving partner or equal relationship; I would become everything I thought they wanted me to be. Almost making them solely reliant on me (co-dependent) to provide and do anything and everything because if they needed me, they wouldn't leave me. Putting their needs before mine and at times not even knowing what my needs were, I was so far down on the list. The fear of rejection or being left because they were too good for me was always there. Through awareness, reading and education, I have recognised that I have been people-pleasing all my life due to fear of abandonment and not feeling deserving of love. I had an anxious attachment style; I had to work hard and earn love because I didn't deserve to receive it freely because I wasn't good enough. I never had boundaries around myself or any partner. As well as feeling this in my mind, it was also in my body. This can manifest itself as chronic pain, inflammation and affects the nervous system or gut. Living in flight, fright or freeze response. Living in a state of fear that this person will leave me, feeling sick to my stomach so many times. I know I have been a very anxious person, overthinking and catastrophising any and every situation in the past. Looking at the worst-case scenario as a protection mechanism.

I discovered the Imperfectly Perfect campaign and podcast around 2020. I was drawn to its rawness and how real and authentic it was in understanding everyone is going through struggles of one kind or another. We see the reels on social media, showing only the highlights and believe this is the whole story when truthfully, we don't know what is really going on. I had hit a personal rock bottom, the breakup with my last girlfriend/fiancée hit me harder than any other, I had thought this was it. A ready-made family and a deep connection with the entire family. It was everything I thought I wanted. When it ended, I had lost all sense of self. I was lost. I decided to seek professional help in the form of a therapist. Something said to me, *It's time to really look at my own behaviours and patterns, I'm in my mid-forties I have nothing to lose*, was my attitude going in, I was ready to do the work and make a shift.

Even though I would blame myself for past failed relationships, it was never solely my fault, of course. However, it certainly was time to take responsibility for my actions. I was understandably a bit nervous going, I had never spoken about my past, my feelings or relationships before this. I broke down in that first appointment and this allowed me to get somebody else's point of view. CBT (cognitive behavioural therapy) was so helpful for me and going back to my childhood and addressing the teenage distorted images I had of myself. The way we talk to ourselves and see ourselves is so important.

A beautiful exercise I was given was to get five people, be it a family member, a friend, someone you know, to write down five words that describe you and it's incredible to see the patterns. Often how others see us is nothing like we see ourselves and usually we are talking down and saying unkind things to ourselves. I think it's important to talk and treat ourselves the way we would treat our loved ones. The beauty in this exercise was to see so many of the same words show up on how others saw me. Even in those past relationships, if my girlfriend/fiancée would have said I was beautiful, I wouldn't have believed it. Only when you finally see your true beauty through acceptance, then you will believe it. I know now that awful feeling of looking at yourself and feeling ugly or unlovable, that is the total opposite to how God sees us.

God has always spoken to me. I had so many times I would get that feeling but couldn't explain what it was! My knowing or my intuition. I slowly but surely found myself. I believe God lives in each one of us and we all have a purpose in this life. I was made exactly the way I was meant to be. Being intentional through my faith and listening to God, I know I am where I was meant to be. I now call myself a deeply spiritual person. During my early therapy sessions, I was asked, 'If there was a blank canvas what would Claire want and see for her future self?' I had no idea because I had never thought about me, only ever what can I do for everybody else, what would make them happy. Thanks to my sessions and my unwavering desire to know and love myself and find my own appreciation of embodiment. I may not know exactly what my future holds but I can say it will be beautiful and I am excited for it. Through one of my favourite spiritual practices, meditation, I have regulated my nervous system. You must go into your body and out of your mind to find inner peace, joy and self-love.

All those years of not feeling enough, now and only in very recent times I can now put the words or have the language to what has held me back most of my life. I have had internalised homophobia. Even admitting this makes me emotional. This, I recognise in myself from hiding parts of my identity, making myself small as to not make others feel uncomfortable around me. A huge sense of guilt has haunted me. I know from my experience this feeling of hiding parts of your identity can truly shape your future and destiny. Worried about how someone may or may not react to you, which is totally out of your control – it is exhausting, you can only control your inner world.

Even in those early years of coming out, I was always concerned how would people react. I would not talk about that part of me, even at external family events, especially if older members were there, again as to not make them feel uncomfortable or they wouldn't understand coming from a different generation, so I better not say anything. This would lead me to form a pattern in my life of having this attitude of how will people react – even if I was to make a friend the conversation in my mind would be this: *If I suggest going for coffee, they might now think I fancy them and it's a date, they will feel really uncomfortable now so I better not do that, as to not put them in an uncomfortable situation.* Now that's not to say the other person ever thought that but that was the conversation in my head. Tied in with my belief of not being good enough, I often would even start a conversation with 'sorry', apologising for even having a voice.

The overriding emotion I felt with this understanding is shame. Ashamed of hiding parts of my identity, not being my true authentic self at times. This feeling would lead me to feel unlovable, looking in the mirror saying to myself, *You are ugly, nobody will love you,* looking back at my relationships feeling like a failure, useless and pathetic if I didn't live up to certain standards. Standards I set for myself that were unachievable for anyone, but if I didn't meet them, I might be abandoned. In society making myself almost invisible, the smaller the better to accommodate everybody else to make them feel comfortable around me.

Then I had a huge breakthrough in seeing myself the way I truly am. Not long ago, my mum sat me down to tell me how incredibly proud her and my dad are of me, I am the best daughter they could have asked for and how I inspire them and other people every day. But seeing me exactly for how I am and the person I have become. I felt so seen and so incredibly loved.

Finally, I can now look at myself in a whole new light. I see that beauty shows up in so many ways. I can look at myself and see the amazing person I am. I am more than a label – so much more, in fact. I have had to overcome so many things and I know all those synchronicities had to happen to get me to exactly where I am today. I am beautiful, kind, compassionate and empathetic in my nature, being told in the past I was too sensitive. I now see this as a superpower, the more I connect with people and speak my truth or be vulnerable, it gives them permission to do the same. I have had some incredible conversations and learning and growing and listening, sometimes that's all somebody wants is for someone to listen. Not to judge or give advice just to listen and say, 'I see you; I hear you.' I see this is a great quality. Allowing God to speak through me and to listen for the next right step for me, so many people don't listen to that inner voice. I have always heard it but certainly when I was younger didn't always listen for it. You get a feeling something doesn't quite sit right but you block it out. The picture I had in my mind of the almost fairytale relationship or the movie where they get married and live happily ever after is just that – a fairytale.

The real work and real life are constant but it's about being consistent and showing up as your best self and learning to love yourself. I feel so empowered now. Looking for external love can only take you so far as I know, if you don't love yourself, you will never be truly satisfied. Surround yourself with like-minded people who lift you up, but also challenge you to grow and be the best version of yourself. Where your attention goes is where energy flows. I have affirmations in my bathroom that I see every day by my mirror that confirm I am worthy, I am lovable, I create my future happiness.

My biggest takeaway is to be your true self, the people who really matter will love you and if people don't appreciate you that's their loss. We should never judge anybody else until we have walked in their shoes; nobody is perfect, far from it, we are all just on this earth having a human experience. I see the awesome person I am with so much love to give. The serendipities of life show up and it's about the journey not the destination. I'm so grateful for my faith, God always had a plan for me. I am grateful for my journey so far, having the awareness to see my truest self and to change my beliefs and live the life I want for me. Changing the narrative about my last relationship from saying it was a failure although it didn't work out, I am so grateful and see the whole experience as a blessing and my biggest lesson. I would have never done the work on myself and would have continued a pattern of people pleasing. My best years are ahead of me. Some people don't ever get this chance so for that I am so excited for the future. This is not to say I won't have many lessons or challenges ahead of me, but with awareness, strategies in place and my faith, I know things will always work out for me.

If I could go back, I would say to my fourteen-year-old self, *Claire, have compassion for yourself, you have the biggest heart, you are unique and beautiful, and you will touch so many people's lives from being exactly who you are. Your most authentic self is more than enough. Love yourself in the same way you love others and treat yourself with kindness and respect too.* A quote I would have said back then would be, 'Don't be afraid to be different, worry about being like everybody else.'

Through my journey of growth and self-love, and living my core values, I see myself as I truly am. A strong, confident, resilient woman who radiates love through kindness and positivity. The funny thing is once you give yourself permission to love yourself, it goes out into the world and without doubt comes back tenfold. Surrounding yourself with positive, like-minded people wanting to spread love and compassion to make the world a better place through the campaign is just a beautiful practice.

If one person can relate to my story, I feel proud to have shared it. Within the LGBTQ+ community, I am proud of how far we have come but there is still work to do. I never take for granted the struggle that has come before me and the privileged world I live in, how I am accepted for being myself, how I accept myself. I hope for a future world of no more stigma around identity and only love and acceptance for humankind. Also, for anyone in general who has lacked self-belief or self-worth. You are valuable, you do matter. You are loved. A society where we can talk about mental health issues in a way where we now discuss and ensure physical health, both go hand in hand. Not one person on this planet hasn't had a bad day or negative self-talk and doesn't need someone to talk to about it. It's okay not to be okay sometimes. Most importantly be imperfectly perfect.

CLAIRE SMITH

Group Fitness Trainer
Connect: @clairesmith6469

JACLYN ALBERGONI
FOUR LESSONS

Things started to fall apart when I was twelve. The day my parents separated. I still remember listening to my mother's cries as I woke one morning. I thought my parents had an argument or something, but to my surprise this was the event that changed the world as I knew it. I was living in Italy at the time, and I was pretty happy there. I had friends, a big house and family. It was my world. What I knew. Never did I imagine that our lives would change so drastically.

My parents tried to protect my brother and me from the truth, but in doing so they never explained anything to us; I guess they never really knew what to do or how to explain the situation to us. They tried to move forward as if nothing had happened, avoiding any type of conversation or confrontation. We obviously knew something was wrong, and it became obvious that day at our family vacation home in Portofino, as we suddenly had to pack up and go back home with no warning. My mother, however, was going to stay behind, which of course I knew was odd. As we were about to drive off, my mother could no longer play along and released all her frustration. She started yelling at my father as we slowly drove away.

My mother was a very sweet housewife and she really loved my father. She did not cope with the separation because her whole life revolved around my dad. When she lost her husband she felt as though she had lost herself, eventually leading her to attempt suicide. Once again, nothing was explained to my brother and me. I realised that my mother was in a mental institution the day we visited her at the hospital. I was told that she wasn't well. So, when we visited her, I thought we were going to see her at the general hospital, but we were taken to a separate building. As we walked into the building, I noticed there was security, we had to go through a locked metal gate to enter the ward, and the weirdest part was some of the patients were walking around talking to themselves. Being so young I still hadn't made the connection until I saw my mother. She looked unrecognisable. I noticed her robe was missing the rope so I asked her, 'Where is the rope for your robe, Mom?' In a dazed, slow-motion horror movie scene she slowly turns to look at me and says, 'They don't allow us to have them here because people try to hang themselves with them.' And that was the moment I understood. Because of her mental state, and also because she had nothing left in Italy, she decided to move back to Australia. So, my brother and I had to go too. I did not want to move to Australia. I wanted to stay with my father, but it was never a choice.

I resented my family. My mother for checking out, my father for not being there and my brother for giving up. Things only got worse as time went on. The family dynamic was completely broken. In my parents' defense, neither of them had exemplary parents themselves. My mother was given up for adoption when she was four years old, and my father's parents were completely absent.

The move was tough. Mostly it was a culture shock. I went from driving my scooter to school, basically living on my own, to a private girls' school where you would get detention for pulling your socks up. On top of all that, I knew how to speak English, but I had to learn how to read and write in English and that was a whole other ball game. I began isolating myself and I was struggling to accept how my life had come to this. There was a lot of fighting in the home, and it became impossible for either of my parents to control me. I was mad, I was sad and I was resentful. I started to self-harm, and on top of that I was at the start of the long journey of my eating disorder. It didn't help that I became friends with two other girls in my school who also were experimenting with purging and extreme dieting. I was developing very bad coping mechanisms to deal with the chaos and intense emotions I was going through. With no support or mentors, I was doing what I could to manage the pain and loneliness.

I felt so alone. I was trying to make friends but at the same time I felt so damaged that I didn't feel as though I belonged anywhere. I would look for any excuse to be away from home; everything there reminded me of what had happened and why I was in so much pain. I also hated school and so I started to skip school.

I started to hang out at this pool hall and that's where I met Joe. He was seventeen, handsome and we just hit it off. The first time I felt seen in a long time and what I thought would be someone who understood me. The first six months of our relationship was so beautiful and romantic. Out of all of the drama and lack of connection I thought I had finally found love! But little did I know that the worst had yet to come. Who I thought was to be the love of my life, turned out to be my greatest lesson on self-respect.

Joe was from a low-class family, father was ex-military, mother was a hypochondriac with two brothers, a younger sister and thirteen cats in a three-bedroom house. With so many issues at home I would basically live between Joe's family house and mine. My eating disorder was in full swing at this stage and Joe started to show his true colours and become extremely abusive. Physically and emotionally. I was so in love, so desperate for love and needed love so badly that I would take it in any form or shape it would show up, even in abuse.

I was in this relationship for three and a half years. Three years of mental and physical torture, and as if that was not enough, I was torturing myself by starving and binging and purging. Abusers will use your weakness to manipulate you, and Joe was no exception. 'You anorexic dog.' 'You are fat.' 'Have you ever dropped a pie, Jackie? That's what you look like when you smile.' 'You look like a half-sucked mango.' 'If you love me you will do this, otherwise I will leave you.'

He did, however, use his abusive ways to save my life. My anorexia-bulimia was so out of control that one morning I collapsed on the floor. My body was so frail that I wasn't able to walk. So he gave me an ultimatum: 'You either eat or I'll break up with you.' You would think that after this many years of abuse and violence, I would leave. It wasn't when he choked me until I passed out or tried to stab me with a kitchen knife or the endless verbal abuse and shame … It was when he betrayed me. Of course he cheated on me! And with none other than my closest friend, the one who I bonded with when it came to giving each other tips on how to purge. At the time, this was one of the most devastating moments of my life. I wanted to die just like my mum. He became my world and I felt as though I had nothing left. Looking back, it was the best thing that ever happened to me.

Lesson one: things that appear to be against you may just be the very thing you need.

I started to pursue acting at this time. And to my luck I got into the Actors Centre Australia. My friend had to basically force me to audition! That's the problem when you have such low self-esteem, you don't believe you can achieve anything. But acting made sense. It was a way for me to process my emotions, understand human behaviour and through that learn how to build some self-respect. Turns out I was pretty good at it and in no time, I built an insatiable lust for it. My obsession for Joe turned into my obsession for acting.

These were some of the happiest days of my life. I remember how excited I was, I felt like I actually belonged and above all that I was wanted. I graduated, got a great agent and was working. Not too long after I booked a guest-starring role for *All Saints,* a popular Australian TV show and soon after that I was a semi-regular on *Home and Away.*

Even though I was doing okay for a while with my eating disorder, it started to get worse as the memories got clearer. I also started to smoke weed daily. This was my way of self-medicating to deal with my depression. My self-soothing habitual routine looked like this: I would go to the gym for three and a half hours, six days a week, and on my way home go by the supermarket, buy as much ice cream and as much junk food I could afford to then purge all day, followed by a never-ending weed session. It was as if I was torturing myself. But I was actually trying to deal with the chaos inside me. There was also a part of me that recognised the injustice and the traumas that I had experienced as a child.

I was getting older, wiser and slowly more able to understand. Because for a while there I did not even realise what had happened. How could I? How could a six-, ten-, twelve-year-old understand? In a way I started to have a little more compassion and wanted to find a better way to live. As much as I was a victim – and by the way I hate that word – I was so far from where I wanted to be, who I wanted to be that I was lashing out. I have to admit that I wasn't always the kindest person. I was rude to customers at a coffee shop that I worked at, I was at times abusive at home, I was aggressive, confrontational and I was not able to manage the extreme emotions I was going through. I was angry. Very angry. I was desperate. Looking back now I can clearly see I was doing what I could to keep going. My anger became my fuel, my way of pushing through. I was always a fighter. Anger isn't a bad thing when it's channelled the right way. Anger can help you make change happen, can push you through the impossible, but when used the wrong way it's like fire destroying everything in its path. But a contained fire can cook food and keep a house warm. All of this made me realise the importance of a support system, a mentor or someone who would have been there to guide me through it all. And I knew I wanted that, but of course I looked for it in all the wrong places.

As time passed, I was still struggling with my addictions, so much so that it was affecting my acting. I was called on set less and less and I couldn't help but let that influence my self-worth. Acting was EVERYTHING to me. It was my link to happiness, to life, to joy … you take that away and you leave me with a void. I started working for a group home for people with disabilities and mental health problems. This place was high security, in a way it reminds me of the hospital where my mother was when I was twelve. The clients were at times violent and were constantly breaking the law, which is why they were there. It was a challenge, and I certainly was not qualified to deal with the extremes of this job, however I think I did okay. You cannot help but have compassion for these people. And oh my! Their personalities were big and loud.

I eventually started to take on more graveyard shifts; I enjoyed the quiet and I did not have to deal with people. Things eventually started to get intense after a shift in management. This caused a lot of problems for the company, the staff and of course the clients. It eventually led to some staff walking off the job in protest. These people had worked there for years, they had established a relationship. As the new management arrived, they were not equipped to handle the clients, partly due to lack of experience with them. There was a change in the clients' medications and this is where the old staff were not onboard. One of the top managers came to visit the home, let's call her Karen. She asked to take the clients out to the backyard, which of course was gated to keep them from running away. I wanted to borrow a chair form the office to sit outside, which made no sense because there was a bench outside. She disregarded the staff's advice and insisted she knew best. A few minutes passed by and Susan went back inside to ask for more cigarettes for the clients. I was stunned 'Where are the clients?' She smiles and says, 'Outside.' I took a deep breath knowing full well what was about to happen. I ran past her and when I got to the backyard there were no clients but a chair was pushed up against the gate where they had successfully executed their escape. Luckily I found one client hiding behind the gate. However, the other was gone. It wasn't unusual for the clients to run away, especially on excursions, but never had they run away from the house. Eventually the client was recovered and returned at 2am on 6 May 2013 by the police. I went through procedure and scanned her with the handheld metal detector wand for any weapons or lighters. Nothing. The client eventually went to her room, and I headed back to the living room to watch TV.

A few minutes passed and the client got up again to go to the restroom and passed by the living room slowly shuffling her feet. Suddenly I hear *BOOOOOOOOM!!!!* I jumped off the couch and opened the door to the hallway to find a huge cloud of black smoke making its way into the living room. 'Shit! FIRE! FIRE! FIRE!' I knew my first priority was to open the back door as we were literally in a cage. So, if something happened to me, we were all cooked. I ran to the back where the client who started the fire was patiently waiting for me to be let out. I opened the gate and looked at her bedroom window. The fire was huge! Even the metal fence next to it caught on fire. I called the police for help but I soon heard screams from inside the house as the other client was still in her bedroom. She was frozen in fear so I had no choice but to go back in. I reached her door, which was right next to the room that was on fire, and tried to encourage her to come out. I tried to open her door, but she had it locked. The smoke was building up really fast. I grabbed my keys and as I was about to unlock the door, the very expensive smoke alarm system decided to fail and suddenly it was pitch black. No exit sign light. Nothing. By this time I was using my shirt to cover my mouth. 'Okay, I need to kick the door down!' I backed away to prepare myself to kick the door and next thing I know I was on the floor. I was so confused as to how I got there. I decided that I had to get out. As I crawled out of the living room it was pitch black, smoke everywhere! I could hear the client screaming for help. Her window cage was supposed to unlock in the event of a fire and therefore she should have been able to jump out.

But we were not that lucky. I went to the window to help her breathe, trying to get the smoke away from her mouth. It was truly suffocating. Both our eyes were burning and the smoke was so thick it was impossible to breathe.

I was so scared that she would die, so I decided to try go back in to help her one more time. As I reach the living room the fire had already reached the hallway and just as I was about to enter *STOP!* I heard this voice in my head, *You won't make it out.* I felt like a coward but I decided to listen and I stepped back out, watching the horror movie unfold before my eyes. I felt so guilty for not being able to help the client. In that moment everything slowed down and a sense of calm suddenly came over me. *This is your sign. You either go and do what you are meant for or it's your time to go.* The police and fire department finally arrived and luckily everyone was rescued.

But I was done. I quit my job, got some therapy to help me recover from that event and packed up to move to LA. The land of opportunity. And the crazy thing is that I wanted to go to LA, but I never had the courage. It took this moment in my life, a moment that could have had a very different and tragic outcome for me to take a leap of faith.

Lesson number two: Don't wait for tragedy to make you step out of your comfort zone.

LA was everything I dreamt it would be. Excitement, adventure and Hollywood. I didn't know anyone, and it took a little time to meet people, but one thing is for sure, it is not hard to meet people in LA. With time and many tries, I eventually got my O1 visa. Meaning I was out of work for a long time and all my savings went to lawyer fees, accommodation and travel. The catch to the O1 visa is that you can only work within your creative field. I was meeting some of the top agencies, thanks to my manger in Australia.

Unfortunately, my manager passed away and any connections in the business he had were suddenly cut off. Meaning I had to start from zero, and somehow get a job! Well, here is the thing, it is almost impossible to find cash jobs in LA. Trust me, I tried! But luck was on my side, and one day at a bar I started talking to this older man who offered me a cash job. Only catch was, well, it wasn't your typical job. I was offered a manual labour job, where I would help restore an old train. Yes, that meant metal and woodwork, and anything that involved hardcore labour. We are talking scraping glue from an entire train cart, wall to wall, coating steel with chemicals, cleaning shards of metal from underneath and inside the train, placing insulation, smashing old wooden floors … you name it.

I would be so exhausted that I would sleep on my lunch hour. Also, the trip to work was no joke, one bus, a train and a thirty-minute walk every day. I would be so dirty that people would stare at me on the public transport.

Eventually I graduated to working in customer service at a few cafes and restaurants. I even worked as a bartender, and still to this day I cannot make a cocktail. I had to do everything I could. I worked myself to the ground, and between the long hours on my feet, earning little money, the stress of constant survival and the increasing abuse of weed, it all led to me having a severe panic attack. I took myself to the emergency room even though I did not have any health insurance. For those of you with free health care who may not know, in the US you have to pay to go to the hospital, doctor or anything to do with health care. I had to make a deposit to prevent receiving a huge bill and I gave up the only money I had saved. I was sent home with some Xanax. I became a shell of a human. I was so down on myself, my dream of becoming an actor was crushed and I was barely able to move out of the bed. I had to pack up everything and move back to Australia to get help. It took me six months to recover. Because I was not going to give up, once I felt better, I decided to pack up again and try one more time. I had to go back. You would think that this event was enough to make me quit smoking, but it wasn't. However, it was definitely the start of recovery.

Therapy was helpful, but once I started to take my spiritual and self-healing practices more seriously that's when my life started to really get better. I was meditating at least once a day, and I was committed to writing a page of affirmations every day. I became obsessed with healing teachers such as Louise hay, Deepak Chopra, Wayne Dyer and Eckhart Tolle. I understood that having another mental breakdown was not an option, especially since I was vulnerable because I had little to no support in LA. More than anything I started to apply the lessons, and started to take a look at myself, my lifestyle choices and what it meant to truly heal. I was so committed that I even started a YouTube channel called the Meditation channel where I created my own meditations. I was simply sharing everything that I was learning myself.

Once I started to feel better, my self-confidence grew and I finally started to look for an agent, manager and go back to acting classes. It was my dream to one day get into the Masterclass at the Ivana Chubbuck Studio and of course start working as an actor again. Things started to look up, I finally changed jobs and broke the cycle of waitressing! I started a new job in San Diego selling solar door to door. Even though that meant it was a five-hour drive every day I was actually starting to make some money, save and afford a few nice things here and there. Didn't matter what it took because I was prepared to beat this! But when did my life truly take a turn? When I looked at what was not working. No matter how hard I tried I was still one step behind ... and I could no longer lie to myself. It was IT, my medication, my escape, my excuse. The weed. I said to myself, *I have to commit to this. If I can commit to one year of sobriety and see if anything improves then I know for sure that it's the weed.* In the end, our energy and thoughts create our reality, I really believe it and I knew that even though things were getting better I was still not where I wanted to be. So, I took a leap of faith. And you know what? It was extremely hard. I mean, I would smoke day and night for years and changing a habit like that takes a lot. But I slowly cut out the tobacco then smoking to vaping, to gummies and finally I was free. And you know what? With time, everything changed. I started earning more money, I got an agent and a manager that lead to an eight-episode for Starz called *Three Women*. I got into the Masterclass and I moved into my dream home, finally got two dogs and now as I am writing this I am one month away from my dream wedding in Italy. I also started to teach meditation to others and run support groups in rehabs, my YouTube channel has four thousand subscribers and I started my own business. I know in my heart that none of this would have been possible if I was still addicted. Above all, my anxiety and depression are gone. I am happy. I am still a work in progress, don't get me wrong, but I am no longer a slave to my past, to my addictions, my fears! I also started to rebuild my relationships with my family. I say all this because it is possible, but it takes consistency, commitment and above all it takes courage.

Lesson number three: Do not seek happiness, seek self-empowerment and self-respect.

Self-empowerment is key. We cannot be happy all the time, life is so unpredictable that we cannot control external events. But you can learn to respect yourself through self-empowerment. When you build yourself back up from the ground, you are building yourself from the inside out and that's when you become a force to be reckoned with. You can have a bad day, but you are less likely to act out because you value the work and commitment you have given to yourself. I have become an advocate on self-empowerment and this is what I teach others. Fighting for the little girl or boy that still lives in you, who needed support, love, protection and to be valued. I no longer wait for the things I need to come to me. I give it to myself. I am my own hero, my best friend and I show up for myself. You have the power to change your life and the only place you need to start is from within. I know it sounds cliché but it makes sense. Look inside and you will find all that you need.

Final lesson: Everything you need is already inside you.

JACLYN ALBERGONI

Actress / Meditation Practitioner / Author

Connect: @jaclyn444

MICHELLE LANGE
INSERT TITLE

I t has taken me half a century and some change to author this story. A story that has certainly become the very fabric of my life and is now my life's work. I use the phrase, 'the fabric of my life', because it brings to life the very essence of my journey, richly infused with what Pierre Teilhard de Chardin said in the *Catholic Thinker:* 'We're not human beings having a spiritual experience. We are spiritual beings having a human experience.'

We are all connected within this 'life' fabric and share commonalities that soulfully bind us. We share an energy that can be an inspiration or hindrance to humankind.

Let us begin with the end in mind, starting with what has brought me to this point, where I share how the fabric of my life becomes connected with yours. My moment of self-awareness began in a bathroom, where I stood performing a breast self-examination, realising in those seconds that turned into long minutes, that the dense breast tissue I felt was no longer dense tissue, but a lump.

Looking in the mirror, I released a sigh, a long sigh followed by a sharp intake of breath to stop myself. Then, like most other times of needfulness, I said a prayer. A prayer that would silently communicate to me from the Divine, God, Source, what I intuitively knew, that I was about to walk into a diagnosis no-one is ever ready for.

Instinctively, I knew that prayer was my 'place' to lament over my findings, create a clearing to ready myself and gain reassurance that all would be all right. I asked God that nothing too overwhelming would arrive in the details of my new normal and that He would be my stead.

Straining my face and whole body so I did not completely break down, I paused as I heard a beloved voice call, 'Mum! Where are you?' I broke from my tearful reverie, wiped my eyes and in true Michelle form – straightened myself up and put on a smile. But who was I kidding? My daughter is intuitive and would surely sense my emotion. How could I keep this from her?

Like she had sensed something amiss, my daughter knocked agitatedly on the door with concern in her young voice, 'Mum, are you okay?'

With effort, I choked out, 'Yes, I'm just in the middle of something and I'll be out in a moment.'

This was the beginning of an arduous climb through struggles that made me feel like I was in a jungle, where challenges felt like vines reaching into the core of my soul, limiting my capacity to create a win. At the time, it was an unthinkable experience and yet here I am, appreciative of life, grateful for my journey and a diagnosis that eventually created healing, learning and strength.

I have had several life experiences that created a protective armour within my soul. These are threads where iron will, resilience, love, forgiveness, hope, joy, kindness, gratitude and acceptance anchored me. Anchors are crucial elements that allow me to 'live into' my cancer with a flow.

The best way to describe a flow is to use the analogy of a river. Flow or energy current within you is like a river – there is perpetual motion. It never ceases, ages or stops unless you create a dam. It will physically manifest itself as feeling youthfully exuberant or enthusiastic, joyful and loving warmth. When you reach a place where you can acknowledge and accept your circumstances, it becomes an inner spark to ignite an even greater positive internal current.

Late September of 2021, the initial visit with my GP confirmed, 'Yes, you have a lump.' Moving quickly to the mammogram, which was going to take two weeks to schedule, there was a remarkable occurrence – an opening five days later! To some this may seem a miniscule thing, but to me it was evidence that God was in the very details of my life from the moment I uttered that first prayer. Can you imagine knowing that you have a tumour growing inside you, yet you must patiently wait to let medical science catch up with your intuition? Patience is not an emotion that was present; need I say any more?

God knew my plight, my way of being, who I had become and who I was meant to become – and so did I. When science and medicine caught up with my intuition, it was an October morning. To my horror, not only did they find the tumour, but they also discovered another. It was devastating to say the least, however, my anchor of gratitude showed up. Let me give you context for this gratitude.

As we were about to finish the mammogram, the tech paused, and I watched her ponder something. She had an aha moment and said to me, 'I know I said we are done; however, I feel like I need to get this one last angle coming from as far back as we can under your armpit.' She was hesitant, understanding my discomfort, because for a moment, I winced. However, that aha moment paid off exponentially.

The tricky thing about this cancer is that early detection is crucial. This scan showed that the cancer had breached my breast and was now in my lymph nodes. Lymph nodes are the superhighway of toxic waste extraction, and they need to function unimpeded. I was devastated. Can you see why the energy of gratitude was needed in this battlefield? In the beginning, I could not use the words 'battle' or 'battlefield'. They were like dirty words to me. As time furiously ticked by, I discovered that cancer is not just about illness, it is about an emotional, spiritual and mental expedition.

Expedition – a journey that is undertaken with a definite purpose. My journey began with promptly finding an energy flow, tapping into my already developed strengths, accepting that there would be weakening (not weakness!) and moving forward with eagerness.

Throughout my life, my path has been strewn with markers, signs and signals from God and the universe that gave me direction and learning. You know, those moments where you felt sure about your gut and instincts? Either I could be open and surrender to it, or close and be stuck holding on to that which was keeping me small, holding me back. Sometimes it was my own doing, my murky mindset filled with the debris of life.

The time had come to do some mindful mindset housekeeping. It became apparent to me, early in my cancer odyssey, that I needed to pay close attention to the needle on the gauge of my life that tracked my energy and its flow. It was counterintuitive to question the fundamentals of my thoughts, feelings and learning, however, after making an initial assessment I found my observation to be self-enlightening. You see, to be aware, you need to spend time in a state of awareness. Self-awareness encourages discovery and discovery welcomes learning – needed insights. The reciprocating cycle, like many others I have found, meant moving beyond a diagnosis, a life change, an archaic thinking or behaviour.

I genuinely wanted to be my authentic self, be positioned BEYOND labels, others' expectations and where the world thinks or has socialised I SHOULD be, given current positioning. Having a profound sense of individualism meant to be true to who I am. Did I know who I was? The age-old question we all at some point ask ourselves, only we do not stick around long enough to hear the answers that follow. A human trait of covering up the mirror, the reflection of untruth we believe, again based on others' proffered opinions.

Dispelling those opinions begins from the inside out. I had many that I held onto so tightly that my burden of choice became heavier than it needed to. I felt a compulsion, just as breathing, to disperse these narratives. I threw caution to the wind and let go, truly trusting myself to travel beyond my past. I had a deep 'knowing' that this is where I belonged, even when I was told that I should not be behaving in a certain way. The external voices of opinion whispered that I should not be so positive or upbeat as if I were insulting the cancer for being so happy and grateful.

Gratitude was the mechanism to raise my brilliance level. We are not discussing intellect, but the internal thermometer of vibration and one's own light. To close this energy path would be inauthentic to the vision of my future self. The self I envisioned healing, not just my body but my soul, heart and mind. That sojourn began as I said earlier – 'trusting myself to travel beyond my past.' The key component in that sentence is TRUST. Trust is a change magnet in everything you do, say and become. To build trust, you need unequivocally a foundation based on genuine character, capabilities/capacities to act with integrity in competent self-belief. Do you believe in you, to bring this character forward without reservation?

My belief, with a smidge of certainty, was that I would live to see many more days. Days that are filled with love, enthusiasm, joy, appreciation, gratitude, forgiveness and being born of light, possessing the energy that is the light of life. Light of life is a vibrancy that engages another anchor of strong threads. These threads create a continuity in my life. They can for you too. Think of it this way ... you are a creation of a lifetime. Every sunset and sunrise ripen the sweet taste of JOY – an inexplicable gift that lifts you above where you were. A flow of energy without judgement or opinion is freeing, not restrictive. This is your birthright and can be called upon at any time. Joy is within you and can decide to hold a place for it.

My path to get to this understanding started in 2005 because that was the year I gave birth to my son, Makaio Ikaika, at twenty-four weeks gestation and weighing under two pounds. Makaio possessed a remarkable spirit and spent his life teaching me to trust my intuition. He helped me see my spiritual strengths and evoke a life-changing perspective that would carry me through what was ahead. You see, dear reader, Makaio lived in this earthly state for thirty-three days. And in his short life span, I experienced the greatest joy, pleasure, hope and sunshine, followed by the deepest darkest storm one would ever be asked to endure.

Endure – there is a phrase that instils a sense of 'keep going' like the little engine that could. Only, in my case, my endurance, my 'could' had run out, like a puff of steam the moment I walked into the NICU. My real life was depicting things we only see in television shows like *Chicago Hope* and *ER* television drama series of our time that we would get sucked into. I was getting sucked into the vortex of reality in a very tangible way, quickly.

There, in the NICU, with exactness and a full measure of love, nurses and doctors huddled around the isolette, rescuing my son. All carrying their share of the load – giving CPR behind a veiled curtain propped between tiny incubators. In the distance, an infant cried, machines beeped. Almost screaming, as I rushed quickly to my baby's side. Overcome by a sinking feeling, all I could manage was to drop to the floor. The deep knowledge from days earlier had arrived without fanfare. This moment left no time to ignore or even argue with it. During this great turmoil, I was betwixt keeping myself together but wanting to collapse, I was a teeter-totter going from, 'I am okay' to 'I am not okay'. The struggle to keep up appearances lost, and my life and my joy emptied in one stealth, silent move.

In a heap of deathly sorry I collapsed like a puddle of water. I dissolved onto the floor crying, 'My son, my baby, NO, NO, NOOOO!' Disbelief raged like an endless storm. The voice of the neonatologist echoed as if from a great distance. 'Call it! Please … Call it!' as she walked away in tears. In a forever while, everything slowed down to a second-by-second scene. Tears flowed like the melting ice in the warmth of spring. My voice, my inner voice, delicately balanced the tightrope wire of grief, knowing at any moment I would be lost in that great abyss like a Greek tragedy, only my life was not a Greek tragedy. My husband, Matthew, was stoic, strong and true to the gentle giant he could be and held me tight and close. His inwardness was experiencing its own deep realisation, crippling him one minute at a time. A psyche juggling act to be strong or give in to the grief. The grief of losing our baby. It takes a remarkably strong man to stand with his wife and keep her up while putting aside his own grief.

Only ten minutes before, we had been on the phone outside the NICU scrambling to get an anointing blessing for our son. The NICU team interrupted our call, asking us to rush back. We scrubbed our hands with purposeful haste.

In a flash my truth had arrived – raw and real. I raised my head to the sky and in my soul, heart prayed, 'God give me strength as I have none. I am undone in the most inexplicable way!'

Before long, I found the courage to rise from the floor. I vaguely heard George, our respiratory therapist, say, 'Michelle, what would you like to do?'

My mind was spinning out of control. You are asking me what I want to do? Are you crazy? I am in the middle of something tragic! I needed to find the pause button quickly. This is too much, too fast. The questions loomed in my head repeating over and over. Again, patiently and with compassion, George asked, 'Michelle, what would you like to do with your time with Makaio?' Finally, I pulled myself into the present, and with fresh courage, wiped my tears, found a chair, sat down and faced George. In scrubs, he leaned over my son like a tower, still giving Makaio life-saving oxygen by hand. George was breathing life into my boy, my Makaio was still very much here, responding, weak, but there.

Gratitude filled my soul. Yes, yes, a moment, a splinter, a sliver of

– not hope, but time. Time was precious and a commodity I needed. Time to reflect, time to decide and time to gather myself together so that I could offer strength to my sweet Matthew who gallantly powered on. This would be a day to remember forever.

As cliché as what I am about to say sounds, this was not my first rodeo when it comes to losing a child. In 1998, I buried Tamati Bryton at a small cemetery in Aramoho, Wanganui, New Zealand. Alone, with three other children to care for, I marched on with a vigorous focus on the beatitudes of gratitude and gladness. I carried my grief the best way that I could, processing in my time and in my way, fully aware that my children had lost their brother and needed their mum. A hard decision – however, wisdom, common sense and instincts prevailed. Life is filled with choices; it is as common as change is present every minute. The choice in front of me was about finding a place for my grief while still being present to my three children without them feeling unseen, unheard and unloved.

In the cold sterility of the NICU unit, I stared at my son, so small and weighing only two pounds. My eyes soaked in his strawberry blonde and black hair, gorgeous blue eyes, big feet, tiny hands holding on to his intubation tube. I knew that his last breaths needed to be taken within the arms of both his father and me, surrounded in unconditional love. What passed my lips, as I said with assuredness was, 'You know, George … Since that moment in July when you scooped up Makaio, I have never held him close to my heart, loving on him. May I hold him please?' Decidedly, I knew that Makaio was going to pass through this life with the whole energy of my heart and soul to guide him tenderly.

The tenderness of a mother and father's touch, to soothe the pain he was experiencing, the gentle soft sound of a nurturing voice singing melodically to fill his tiny ears. The whispers of love and devotion of a mother and father. Delicately, his tiny hand curls around our fingers. The incandescent smell of his newborn fragrance filled our nostrils. My gesture to love Makaio in his last moments, ironically, became his banner of love to me – his epitaph to hold me up in the months that followed his passing. It would awaken my soul.

A choice had to be made to either keep trying to save our son, or to let him go like the sunset of a spent day. The quality of life for Makaio was diminishing quickly as each minute went by. His oxygen and heart rate stats were dropping to an alarming level. With each alert, there was a change. Let me pause for a moment. Hard and serious life decisions, especially this kind, take faith, courage, understanding, compassion and an energy flow that inspires what I call 'realistic positives'. Soul-to-soul, spirit-to-spirit connectivity nestles amidst the ego of motherhood – created to protect, love, nurture and save those born from love.

I mentally prepared myself, attempting to overcome my instincts, to put aside my will to decide what to do. I had to decide – what is the higher good for my son? What would his quality of life be? Could he survive the elevated levels of antibiotics without becoming deaf? Would the high saturation of oxygen blow out his retinas? This was a defining instance when I had to selflessly see what future struggles he would have – should he survive.

Nestled to my breast, I slowly rocked him as George bagged every breath. How was I going to help Makaio live into the end of his life? Live into the end of life means making Makaio's physical environment as comfortable as possible. Having his team help us make choices that enabled Makaio to be pain-free as much as we could. Being there to provide physical touch as comfort. Deciding for another, to live or not to live, is insanely challenging, rigorous and complicated, to say the least. The most loving gift, the most loving kindness, honour and choice I could make as his mother, his steward of life, would be to let him go.

As the minutes ticked by, there was a sense of peace. For a second, I felt like a lone bubble meandering across the sky on the wisp of a breeze, without a care. I looked at my son, nestled my face close and murmured in his ear, 'I love you, my peanut – so very much.' Most unexpectedly, our souls seemed to collide as one, knitted together in harmonious felicity when a message communicated from his heart to mine rang with clarity like a chiming bell. In the still of my mind, I heard … as his soul was speaking to mine, *Mum. Mum, I love you. I am going to be okay. I promise. Mum, you can let me go. I know you love me, but it is time. Mum, it will be okay.* In a twinkle, those soothing whisperings brought calm and peace.

Looking toward Matthew, I could see that he knew just as I did. With a reassuring nod, he lifted his hands for me to walk Makaio to his big, warm, welcoming and comforting arms. Within that place one could find a serene tranquility. I kissed Makaio lightly on the cheek, rose from my chair and with all the courage I could muster, ushered my son to his father, who took the strained mantle from my shoulders. Together, within a symphony of our love, we took our son away from the noise of the unit. He passed peacefully in the arms of his father who, with the greatest strength and reverence, watched over his son's last minutes. Our story of love is memorialised in our hearts forever.

The fabric of my life was stained and strained under the weight of life changes that were like massive boulders. How was I going to get over, under, around and through this? Did I want to get through this? I did not want to get through anything. My self-love died with my son.

Gripped by debilitating depression, I sought to take my life several times over in the next eighteen months. I was in and out of acute care, skirting the system and not coming to terms with where I stood. I was up to my hips in the mud and deluge of a mental health disorder that I did not want to acknowledge. Why? Because the words from a lifetime and generation ago reverberated in my memory banks – 'It's all in your head, just put a smile on your face and everything is going to be alright.'

Everything was not alright because, after the flowers, the goodbyes, the funerals, the many conversations, the visitors – one thing remained the same, me. I was alone, squandering away time in my head with endless wishes from a heavy heart that I could just disappear, every day. I would not advocate this thought process for anyone. However, it was inevitable for me under the circumstances. I was moving fast down a slippery slope. I was lost in my grief, disbelief and shame. Shame and guilt that I had not done enough as a mother. That I had not done enough of anything. I was beating myself up from the inside out with a heavy bat. Life, by my own choosing, was dark and dreary in the worst way.

Talk about life pancake-stacking! One event after another, piling on each other without room to process, figure out and draw conclusions. The universe was sending me all the signals; however, I was not willing to receive them. I had closed myself off from all of life's joys, happiness and hope, and all I received was the dark, dank, ugly, self-histrionics of grief.

Melodrama is what I chose to live into – overpowered and overwhelmed in grief. I wanted to find the words and speak out. I needed to be seen but was forgotten and dismissed. Love became hurt, hurt became rage – rage followed betrayal. Grief was the monster in charge, and it was serving up a large dose of misunderstanding followed by denial.

At the edge of another life cliff I stood, only this time, it was decision time for myself, my condition of life, my future. From a hospital room, I found solace. When I finally allowed myself some serious reflection, I realised that I was unwell. I was suffering from an illness called major depressive disorder brought about by cold, hard life events that I could not predict nor control. In the serenity of that knowledge, I surrendered my soul to God and to myself, accepting that I MATTERED. My life MATTERED and the catalyst for change was the olive branch of the reminder that my son lived his last moment fighting to give me love, to share who he was with me. I could not let his life or the gift it gave me be for naught – for nothing.

Let us go back to the beginning … I have been living this story for half a century and some change … why this story, my story needs to be shared with you. In the shadows of grief, life experience, hardship – I have always found light. My stage-three cancer was to become a stretch of time that culminated in putting to the test all the enlightenment I had gathered. A time and my season to fully embrace. E – enfold energy, M – mindfulness, B – balance, R – real resilience, A – altitude of gratitude, C – channel choices, E – every day ... and surrender.

Surrender to accept what you cannot control and what you can control is your response, accumulation of knowledge, call to action from newly acquired learning and attitude. The following words are those written in real time during this excursion of life, my life.

From my pen to your heart, selected writings of a soul who conquered cancer.

Choices are the ingredients of your perspective, then and now and in a future energy state. Love the journey but most of all love yourself every witt. Meaning – get noticeably clear with yourself, your intentions, who you are and what principles, values now serve you best. This includes those parts of you that you may not like so much. Give those parts of imperfect imperfection to whomever you acknowledge as your higher power. Let go, surrender, fully trusting that divine power has your back. In surrendering our will, ourself, with complete trust, we will move into an emplacement of energy, passion, purpose that you can share with others, most especially yourself – your most valuable soul currency.

There will be ebbs and flows which will necessitate framing one minute to the next. Creating this will allow peace, ease to find that one constant love, coupled with your faith and belief in you to get through those spurts.

To believe in you is to know that ... You are loved, have worth, are enough, even the size if that belief starts as a size of mustard seed, which comparatively is exceedingly small as far as effort. A speck, a pinhole proportion of belief without doubt or compunction. The matches that fuel the inner soulful fire. A fire, that you can choose to let it, will burn from the inside out. This is and will be seen by others as light, inspiration, strength during this your grand tour and no-one else's!

Seek your truths that resonate with your soul and heart. There are many who will say much to do about nothing, creating confusion in you as to what path to take and theirs is the best solution. Trust your gut. As Oprah says, 'You know your gut better than anyone else.' Feel your truth and empower that disposition of you. In the quiet, stop and take time to listen for inspiration, deep knowing to guide you. Nourish your intuition and instincts by following those gut level calls to action.

Selflessly pour into yourself, trusting that as you do so, all that you need is already inside you and with certainty will show up.

Lastly go B E Y O N D with etheric creativity in your pocket.

B – Beauty belongs within the self.

E – Echoes a soul's endurance.

Y – Youthful childlike exuberance to believe.

O – Omniscient GOD.

N – Navigation found in faith filled direction from a soulful place.

D – Daring to dream beyond your wildest divine imagination.

PS, I CAN CERTAINLY WIN EVERY DAY WHEN I CONNECT WITH MY SOUL LANGUAGE POWERS. I went beyond and found myself. I am unapologetically grateful for the lessons that cancer taught me – M xx

MICHELLE LANGE

Connect: mlange@creativebizinc.com

ROXANA POPET
TWO WORLDS COLLIDE

'’ve always had a double life. Always in-between. Never settling in one place and never believing there is this thing called 'home' or 'family'.

They say that what you seek is seeking you, but I was never seeking anything, really. I was trying to run away from it all, to numb the pain that I got so used to, that I believed got imprinted into my being. What was I supposed to do? Not show my emotions or my real feelings, as this would be a sign of failure, defeat and weakness.

And even if I wanted to, I couldn't. I had no idea and no concept of my being. My mind used to be defined by confusion, fear and so much hatred. This great hatred that I had bottled up until recently was towards myself. For not being good enough, intelligent enough, pretty and interesting enough to do anything that would be satisfying to the people around me. I would always look for exterior validation and I became the best people pleaser you could ever find.

It all started when I was just a few months old, when I was suddenly, brutally and unexplainably taken from my mother who was breastfeeding me to live with my grandmother in the village. I don't recall this episode vividly, but it was the first time when I died emotionally, and I actually thought I died for good. Little did I know that many more 'deaths' were about to follow. As I have a daughter myself, I can only imagine the pain and the torment that my mother felt and I can barely imagine mine ...

Growing up in the countryside in the communist era with my grandparents and having my parents visiting occasionally, I became that person that I thought I should be so proud of: 'flexible'. Meaning that I would never ever show my real emotions, intentions and thoughts, as I would be seen as 'weak', 'stupid' and 'extravagant' and I would never be permitted to have a different opinion than the person I was talking to.

Life in the countryside was very beautiful and simple, on one hand. I learned gardening and milking cows and goats and I would help my grandparents around the house and in the fields. We'd get the crops ready in April, pick plums in August and beans and corn in September. On the other hand, as the village community was rather small and everyone knew their neighbours pretty well, I felt great shame and guilt if I'd do anything to bother or upset them. I felt that I should never stand out, or else I'd be judged and laughed at by the community.

'Never stand out and never disagree with them.' But in exchange, let's judge them fiercely. No-one must know our real thoughts and intentions, or else they'll use them to their advantage. Hiding my real feelings gave myself a false sense of power, control and more than anything, it severely affected all interactions. I would always have a mask in public and tried to behave and act in a way that would be pleasing to the exterior. It never even crossed my mind that I needed to feel good about myself or enjoy what I'm doing. I felt as if I was designed for the 'exterior'.

Which was my real face? I never knew, as I had put so many masks on, that I had no idea who I was anymore. But I played along in this scenario that I never understood. I got more confused and I didn't have any goals. I remember being very introverted, but always trying to portray a 'perfect' picture of myself so that I would never be judged. The exterior world seemed very dangerous, frightening and fake to me, full of lies and masks. I thought that everyone had a hidden agenda! The thought that I'd be judged, mocked or looked at in a certain way produced great anxiety for me.

I was barely surviving, but I didn't know it. I literally thought that this is how life is supposed to be. My anxiety level would skyrocket every month, as I would add more anger, frustration and pain on top of feeling invisible, misunderstood and ignored, because I didn't know any way out of that vicious circle.

So here I am in my early twenties, with no understanding of life, love or of my own being. I only knew fear and anger. This is what I translated from all that I was taught growing up: the world is a bad place where you have no chance. Unless you steal, cheat and wreak havoc. At the same time, I wanted to make an impact. To do good in this world and to be a part of something bigger. Needless to say, this would not happen at a regular job. At the same time, I feared rich people. I thought they were criminals and their wealth was only based on stealing. A great conflict around money arose, as I needed money, although I feared them deeply. This thought only created more torment and confusion in my mind, as I had no idea how I'd ever achieve anything of impact. It all seemed beyond overwhelming and I'd juggle between giving up and then finding ambition to dream again.

What do you do when you're incredibly stubborn? Ignore your feelings because of fear, which only added more frustration, self-judgement and anger. I remember that at one point, after the original six months of enjoying my job, I felt really desperate, as I saw no way out: I wanted the money and the privileges offered there, but at the same time, I felt like the ultimate robot, always doing the same thing every day and not being able to leave the office. I felt stuck and truly scared. That was not the place where I can make an impact! Many conflicts have risen in me: Will I be the laughing stock of my family and friends, for giving up on the monthly salary? So many would want my job! What will I do next, anyway? I might as well just be quiet and continue. What will my parents think? What if everyone will judge me and then ignore me for making the worst decisions ever?

I started burying everything deep down, as I would call myself a chameleon, a flexible, 'strong' woman that thought that 'everyone has it hard', anyway. I began taking comfort in the thought that life is really tough for everyone and there's nothing that I can do about it. We need to struggle; we each have something that keeps us up at night. It was all I knew and all I saw around me. I was lying to myself completely and the more I did that, the more my decision-making got affected, as I didn't trust myself that I could get my life back in order ever again. I felt like I lost in life already.

Until one blessed day – and I do consider it blessed – when I found a nodule in my throat during a casual checkup. Fear and desperation deepened. Many treatments and many checkups followed, taking my family through an unimaginable turmoil. And it was just the beginning. More nodules in my breasts, severe skin issues and the 'biggest' issue of them all: a heart condition at twenty-six, tachycardia.

How is this even real? It can't be! I was beyond confused and I felt like I died again and again every single day. Every morning felt like a living nightmare and I don't know what kept me going through all the emotional pain.

I was anxious, frustrated, angry, furious and raging on life, on the people around me, both trying to pretend that I am strong, but who was I kidding, really? I was kidding myself and I didn't realise that I needed to stop punishing myself for not being 'proper', 'bright enough' or 'good enough' for anything and anyone. I would always feel completely powerless. Nothing seemed to work anymore and deep down I know that I had given up on life. That feeling would be consuming me to the core, as I still wanted to live, but not like that! If I had had a reset button, a 'start all over again' option, I would've felt like I'm in heaven! I needed an easy way out. I didn't have the strength to go within, not yet.

My body was screaming at me from the top of my lungs to stop being so negative, so judgemental and so fearful, and to start accepting my emotions, my imperfections and all my mistakes. Back then, mistakes seemed destructive to me! When I'd make a mistake, I'd have panic attacks and my heart would be spiralling out of control, knowing that I am a complete failure and not worth anything.

What was my purpose, what was really the purpose of it all? It all seemed like a waste of time and energy and the mental pain was too strong to handle, as I was navigating in-between two worlds. I could not connect to my emotions and although I could feel pain, I never allowed myself to understand what I was really missing. What did Roxana truly need? Was it love? Compassion, attention, that I needed to give to myself? Looking back, I just needed a break from my negative thoughts. I needed to know that making mistakes is the most natural thing on Earth. I also needed someone to tell myself: 'It's okay and it's only going to be better.'

What I did in exchange was to continually ask for exterior validation and to constantly please everyone around me, as more self-loathing was building up. Looking back, I am astounded of how much hatred and fear I could contain in my system and I am truly thankful that I didn't develop even more serious health conditions, as the intensity of it all seems beyond unbearable now. It felt as if an avalanche of negativity and hate had started to swallow my entire life and all I could do was run.

Of course, I was not at all coachable. On the contrary, I still knew it all and knew it better than anyone would ever cross my path. You couldn't tell me anything! I had all the answers, but in fact, I was just a lost child that lacked guidance. I felt like I lost myself completely and I was wandering on empty streets, vulnerable, frightened. All these experiences got me to feel 'weird' growing up. I felt like I never belonged anywhere.

I had a tough time communicating and building real connections of any sort. My view of the world seemed distorted, as when I got employed, I felt I had no values, no respect for anything and anyone around me and I always believed that I was entitled. I would make huge efforts to go through the day. My ego took full control and I created a false identity just to get by. Although it was a shallow identity, it was all I knew and could process. And it got divided in two: a side that I would present to the world, happy, cheerful and in control of it all, and one that was inside me, the real image of myself, full of fear, hatred and anger.

Narcissism got to be a big issue and I began having problems with anger control. Who was I really, deep down? At this point, I was afraid to even think about it. My narcissist behaviour would give me that dose of instant and deep contentment through getting very angry at my boyfriends over nothing. Anger would consume me completely. I felt that I couldn't do anything about it, as I'd feel like a volcano erupting that would destroy everything in its path.

The pain got so strong, that I got relief through addictions to porn and sex. I needed stimulants right now. Pleasure, right now. Something to make the pain go away at least for a few seconds. But this wasn't real fulfilment, as I would feel even more empty and shallow after the original high feeling. And then I'd be even more in pain. It was a devastating feeling, as each time I felt like I would lose myself even more, although I felt beyond lost already!

What would make me feel better would be the attention from men. I needed to feel desired and to have sexual favours from them, as this would make me feel validated as a woman. I felt like I wasn't worth anything, so I might as well look good and then hopefully men will be impressed. By connecting with them, I'd have a sense of self-worth.

Early in 2022, as I saw the quote: 'The least interesting thing about you is your body,' my mind started to understand the direction of my growth: finally beginning to accept and process my addictions and to see men as human beings with emotions. I was under the impression that men had no feelings and that if I'm not one step ahead of them and use them, they'd do that to me.

My idea of love, sex, men and relationships got distorted to such extend that I began to loathe men from all my heart. I would see them as sexual objects that need to be punished for existing. This hatred created some of the most toxic environments that I could have ever been in. Looking back and being honest, I see that I was the toxic person, making these people suffer tremendously.

I thought that I had fallen in love with my boyfriend, but in reality, when things didn't go my way and when he didn't comply to my needs on the spot, we'd have great fights. It would be a vicious circle of me being in pain, then having revenge on him, not letting him go and threatening him, hurting him again and it would start all over again. As only when I would make him cry, hurt him and say mean things and manipulate him, only then would I feel a sense of false fulfilment. But to me, that lifestyle was all I knew.

I needed to make men feel at least a small part of the pain that I had already been feeling inside for such a long time. That pain would consume me entirely and it would make me do and say many reckless things that I later regretted. 'Hurt people hurt people' for sure.

I knew I needed help, I couldn't live like this anymore! However, I still didn't do anything about it, nothing concrete. I would have talks with my friends at work, complain a lot, but I was still not coachable at all. I just needed people to listen to my problems. I would never do anything wrong and others were always to blame. I had a low and negative opinion about everything and everyone. Everything still looked like a bad joke to me. All was 'nonsense'.

What did I believe in back then? Shallow beauty. I strived for a pretty face and an attractive body, because this was all that I thought I was worth and that I can control. As I couldn't touch any side of my interior being, all focus was on the outside.

I'd let myself be fooled by the beauty of make-up and how it could cover up everything. But even when I had the best make-up on, I still felt highly anxious and completely miserable. I was distracted from myself and I looked for ways to punish myself. This is how many of my romantic relationships looked: punishments. I was not connected to any of my emotions.

And I had these thoughts of, *What's the use anymore?* I'd see a tram going by and I'd wonder what it would be like if I were not alive anymore. This was beyond frightening. Because deep down I wanted to live! I wanted to be brought back to life, somehow, but I wasn't willing to do any work to make it happen, as it all hurt too much.

I soon had to realise the shocking truth that no-one would be there to save me. No-one is going to get me out of the job that I loathed, out of the dissatisfying relationship and no-one will create my goals for me. And it scared me even more, because I had no solution to anything. I was too caught up in my mind to see anything other than my own thoughts which I had completely identified with.

One day, as I kept lingering on the thought that I can't continue taking the same medication as my grandma, one of my friends from work told me how she had cured her breast cancer through neurolinguistic programming. I had never in my life heard of anything like that, but the fact that my friend was cured got my attention. Deep down, what I really felt about mindset was that it's mumbo jumbo, as I already 'knew everything there is to know'. You couldn't teach me anything new.

My friend insisted quite a bit until I got to attend a workshop with my future NLP mentor. I was put in the spotlight in front of the class, answering some questions about my health. It started to slowly make sense how my emotions create my health conditions or destroy it. After that workshop I felt a great change in my body and in my mind and I remember feeling lighter and with more hope for the future. I began seeing my fears in a different light.

My breaking point happened when one day as I finished work, I went to the pharmacy to get my heart pills. And they were the same type that my grandma was taking for her heart condition. And somehow, it hit me:

What has my life become? Will I get to live in my thirties? How did I even get to this point in my existence? And the most frightening thing of them all was that I had no answers to any of my questions.

Through a divine miracle, I eventually listened to my friend and I did my first eight-day NLP course. All the emotions that I unravelled seemed surreal. As I began to loosen my emotional faucet, I remember looking at myself in the mirror and staring into my eyes, as I couldn't believe I could feel my body in a different way. It was such a new experience! I came back a different person and everything changed in my life. I felt great relief. I had actually met my future husband at that course and I began feeling a different connection to men. My healing started and as my relationship with my husband developed, he needed a lot of patience with me still. Things started to feel much better inside, my health improved, but there was still a lot to work on. It was just the tip of the iceberg, but I was ecstatic.

Shortly, still having a mindset of running away from my problems, we moved to Belgium. One part of me was missing Romania, one would loathe my origins, as I would also think that it lacks possibilities to fully develop. And there was another side of me that couldn't accept that I was coming from the village to move to Belgium, and I had quite some conflicts about settling somewhere and having the feeling of 'home'. I felt I didn't deserve to be there.

Up until last year, in 2022, on 26 May, I still felt disconnected from myself at certain levels. Although I had more than ten years of personal development behind me, a beautiful family and a daughter, my ego was skyrocketing, as I felt confused about the business world, about my mission and how to make an impact. It was all new, and while it excited me tremendously, I was both very frustrated.

When Glenn Marsden began to talk, I would really listen! Something felt different. He spoke right to my heart and everything that he said made so much sense, finally! That was one emotional podcast episode, and all the tears took me to a whole new level of healing and relief.

The more I embraced the fact that I simply can't handle my ego on my own, as it got too big for me to even see it anymore, the more I understood the power of asking for help. At first, I would still say: 'Oh, well, who needs to stand out, anyway?' and, 'Why would I put myself under more change and pressure again, since I have already done so much work on myself? Will it ever stop? I literally had enough by now!' without understanding that life itself is a series of continuous lessons. When I stop learning, I stop evolving.

What impacted me at the Imperfectly Perfect Campaign was the power of stories. And as I began to follow Glenn closely and put into practice his wisdom that seemed so relatable, I completely understood that I don't know … what I don't know and that I can't see what's behind the scenes in people's lives. This helped me tremendously understand how ego really works. I got curious to find out how people are really doing and to look at them beyond the flesh and accept their imperfections more. I understood that a highlight reel bears no substance. I only see what people allow me to see. This got me to judge people less and I became more tolerant.

But in order to accept people as they truly are, I needed to do this for me first. I contemplated the idea of working on my ego so much, that I began having different thoughts for the first time, as Glenn's content showed me a different version of 'reality'. I felt inspired! A great reminder for me that each of us has their own reality and I need to be kind to everyone.

What followed was the breakthrough from my make-up obsession and the healing for body dysmorphia. These were tough experiences, but so much needed. I was once attending one of Glenn's live IG sessions and at one point, he said: 'Roxana, come join me live.' The extreme panic that I felt, since I was not having make-up on, and I was also not 'properly' arranged to be on camera, especially live, cannot be described! I felt great anxiety the more Glenn insisted. I was franticly looking for an excuse: *I can't come live with you, since I am about to die!* or, *I am passing out as we speak, and I can't join you!* were my thoughts on the moment. Such extreme anguish, for nothing actually ... Because I eventually joined, and after a few minutes, I felt alright and I realised that literally nothing bad was going to happen! What a major break-through! A fantastic lesson that no-one judges me but me. And I felt it viscerally this time.

This pain and terrible anxiety that I felt was the ego, nothing more. I realised that nothing hurts but the expectations of the ego that I put on people, experiences and more than anything, on me. The era of deep transformations did not stop there. I started having breakthroughs each day. I felt like a child that was discovering the world all over again!

The most impactful breakthrough of my life naturally followed: the humbling exercise with Glenn. I understood what's fully important for me and I could painfully regroup myself with myself, as this exercise got me to imagine that I was on my death bed, saying my final words to my family. I get chills even now as I think about it. This is that type of men-toring that elevated me, enlightened me and opened my eyes to life. I felt deeply transformed.

Since that divine day, as I began having more and more breakthroughs, there was still an ounce of pain in my system. I began fluctuating from ego to heart, heart to ego and I began observing myself when I would do that. Some even more amazing breakthroughs followed and the more I would observe, read and listen to Glenn talking from his heart, about the importance of building heartfelt, honest connections and a powerful community, the more I knew I wanted to share my story in this incred-ible group project.

The ultimate healing for me is happening right now, as I write these lines in my story. The cherry on top of my personal development. As I get to share my story with you publicly, I feel that I have now finally embraced who I am completely.

I am no longer in need of exterior validation and my relationship with men is healing. I learned that everything that I need, I have to offer it to myself first.

I am accepting my feelings and fears, as I am the only one validating my emotions and experiences. Because I know that the outside world is a mirror of my inside world. I accept my mistakes, I apologise and then I do better next time. I know there's much more to learn, which makes me truly excited for the future. Knowing that I am always making the best decisions feels so relieving: I either win or learn. A great life motto.

The world around me is a mirror. Knowing this and having the ego closely observed, I focus on self-love and am patient with and accepting of myself. Having a loving husband that supports me and a loving family seemed like an impossible dream a while ago. It astounds me how I am finally opening up to love and how I am de-numbing myself after so many years.

I learned to embrace the two worlds that I used to live in. I first made peace within them, as there were great hurricanes on each side. I then created one big world from the two.

A great breakthrough for me now is that I realise how vital it is to share my story.

To use my voice and to let it all out. To remember that my being, by design and by default carries great value and when I share my story, I transform the world, as I will never know the impact of my words and experiences for someone that was longing to hear them. I can now see myself as being the person that I wish I had the support of when I was young. And this gives me great power. I am proud of my origins and proud of the person I was, am and will be.

ROXANA POPET
Fear Specialist
Connect: roxanapopet.com / @roxanapopet

KIM SOMERS EGELSEE
MY JOURNEY WITH BREAST IMPLANT ILLNESS

'**G**o from being a glimmer of light to a beam of shining light! Let out who you are and radiate it out to change the world.'

Could this really be happening to me? I'm vibrant. I help teach people to be more confident, happy and positive. I am a happily married woman with two amazing daughters and a career as a life and business coach, intuitive, author, podcast host, TEDx speaker and more. I love my life. I am constantly travelling, attending concerts and having fun. What are these insane symptoms? Why do I feel like I am falling apart? Why are there no answers? Little did I know that in 2023 I would learn that it was breast implant illness, a little talked about wide range of extreme symptoms that develop in those who have breast implants. I had mine for fifteen years. I had no idea that they were poisoning me.

When I was a child, teen and young adult, I never won awards, was the last to get picked on teams, didn't get recognition and really felt I wasn't exceptional at any one thing. I just saw that I was pretty good at a couple of things, and that maybe that was me, and how it would always be. It used to make me a bit sad. However, I continued to study, work on myself and move forward. I worked as a waitress while chasing an acting career, worked as a model, actor, movie and television extra, host, at gyms, sang back-up in a rock group, did some producing and some public relations and marketing and more. I worked in the field of special education both with adults and with children as a teacher and felt very good about that, but still didn't feel in my purpose completely.

I had several periods in my life when I hit bottom and climbed my way out. I met and worked with different mentors. I sifted through several friendships, making sure they were a positive influence. I remained positive, believing in myself and dedicated to stepping into my true life's purpose. I had spent over thirty years studying Jim Rohn, Og Mandino and other personal development greats. I had my college degree, credentials and experience, and with the encouragement of several mentors, began life coaching on the side. As I remained open to my purpose soaring in, I started studying with a transformational teacher named Niurka, getting certified in NLP and supreme influence. I had a huge breakthrough and realised that teaching others to live extraordinary lives was my true purpose, and it all was fuelled from there. I woke up one day, realising and knowing I was 100% in my passion and purpose and it was spectacular. I spoke at events and coached people. I refined my speaking by saying yes to many exciting events, asking for chances to speak and creating my own opportunities and jumping into them – which included hosting and leading hundreds of workshops, meetings and events This has all paid off and my life has shifted to a very fulfilling level. I have now won ten awards in the last few years for my connecting, writing, coaching and speaking; a far cry from my childhood winning nothing. I did a TEDx talk, co-hosted an international show, wrote several number-one bestselling books and much more. I am constantly speaking, coaching and writing aligned with my life's purpose. This has been a lifelong build-up of knowledge, experiences, wisdom, mistakes, successes and study. Finally my purpose and passion was born, fuelled and is flying high. Go for your dreams. Stay in strong belief in yourself and your visions. Believe you will get there, and go far. I hope this chapter shows that there are extreme highs and lows in life, but it is what you do with them that counts.

'What a relief; all humans go through stuff. You're not alone. Realise that you are never the only one. At times, everyone has felt guilt, shame, vulnerability, deep sadness, confusion, anxiety and fear. The key is to pray, read, ask for help, see a coach or therapist, talk to a friend, journal go out in nature and keep moving forward with the knowingness that this will turn into wisdom, strength and bravery.'

In 2008 I was modelling, singing in a rock group, hosting events and I had just had my daughter Noella. After breastfeeding almost two years, and then stopping, my breasts looked kind of deflated. I had gotten used to wearing certain clothing and just had insecurities about having small breasts. At the time, it was out publicly that saline implants were very safe and that having breast implants was an easy procedure. I had a bunch of friends who had done it so I decided to get them. I had the surgery with a quick and pretty easy recovery.

Having new bigger breasts was a big confidence booster for me. I was going to Playboy mansion parties, singing for Ujena swimwear in Mexico, modelling bikinis and wearing things that were harder to wear before. Through the years, it just felt natural like they were my own.

In 2008, I also began studying and getting certifications in spiritual and personal development, life coaching and hypnotherapy. Throughout this process, I began to realise that some of the things that had occurred when I was a child had created a decrease in my confidence. I had experienced a few instances of bullying in both fourth and fifth grades that affected me more than I realised. Thus, lowering my confidence. When I was nine years old I had a lot of friends in the neighborhood that I played with. I was a leader, coordinating shows with all the kids, having meetings in the clubhouse my Grandpa made for me and creating games for the kids to play.

There was one girl that I would hang out with that was pretty mean with an attitude problem and would get her power from being a bully to others. She was one of those people who chased and created drama. Of course, I thought hanging out with her was exciting and made me also feel kind of powerful and rebellious, which is exciting when you're a kid. We would do crazy things like break eggs in people's mailboxes and play ding-dong ditch. Coming from my normal family and home where I was an only child and had a lot of stability, I felt excited being with her … even though I had that strange feeling inside that this wasn't good decisions or behaviour I was choosing. Finally, like all dramatic and rebellious people, the relationship took a turn one day and this so-called friend went from being sweet and fun with me to turning on me in a very mean way. 'Don't you know no-one likes you anymore?' she suddenly told me. She began spreading rumours that were untrue about me and what I was saying and doing around our community and friends. This caused every single other kid in the neighbourhood to turn their back on me, make fun of, yell at and abandon me. I went home crushed, crying and feeling completely abandoned and alone.

Another incident at school at age eleven happened when the boys in my sixth grade class had the girls line up in a row based on how good-looking they thought we were. They went girl by girl and ended up choosing me as one of the last girls, which basically meant that they thought I was ugly. I felt a lump in my throat, like I wanted to run away and go home. Instead, I put on a brave face and sucked in my tears. These two are just a few among many times as a child and teenager where I lost my full power, which added to confidence and self-esteem issues.

I let my positive power be taken away. Instead of dealing with how I felt, or at least talking to my parents or journalling, I kept it to myself and became a people pleaser, hanging onto friends and doing what made them happy so I wouldn't have to ever lose a bunch again. I went above and beyond trying to look beautiful, and started wearing make-up at age twelve, colouring my hair at age thirteen and dressing overly sexy.

Attention made me feel pretty and liked. Little did I know that this type of behaviour was a result of the self-esteem-destroying incidents that had occurred that I hadn't dealt with.

Those were just a few of the times where my power was taken away. I was living to please others. I was not following my heart. I went on like this until at age nineteen, I began dating a very popular guy I had had a huge crush on all throughout high school – he was good-looking and cool. I had even named my goldfish after him in the past. I was so thrilled that he liked me that I jumped into a relationship with him. Very quickly there were warning signs that I had made a big mistake. He was extremely jealous, started to get really mean over small things and even became verbally abusive, calling me horrible names. He also was a very obvious compulsive liar. What was I doing? I put up with it and made excuses for him, even creating a chart of the total number of days we didn't fight. I wouldn't listen to friends and family members that told me to dump him. I began to feel sad and negative more often and it definitely began affecting my confidence.

I started to feel very opposite to the powerful positive person I really was.

I felt powerless and stupid for even being involved in this situation; but little did I realise it had become my project. I was trying to fix him. One night when we went out for my birthday, a guy flirted with me at a restaurant and my boyfriend got so angry with me that he actually hit me, and I ended up jumping out of our car while it was moving. Enough was enough ... But I still didn't learn and just kept on trying to fix him and change him, until I noticed that he had a gambling problem. We had been saving money up to take a vacation to Mexico together and he ended up gambling all of the money away, including my money that I had saved for months. One night we got into such a dramatic fight that we began screaming and throwing things at each other and the neighbors called the police on us.

The two policemen banged on the door and threatened to arrest us if we didn't stop. I felt shocked. *How did I get myself into such a dysfunctional mess? Was I addicted to the drama or trying to fix someone?* It all went downhill from there. There were arguments, fights, lies, a night I got so angry I ran into the street with cars coming. I knew it had to end. I was so done with the relationship but each time I tried to leave, he would threaten to kill himself.

Finally, I just couldn't take it. I wasn't responsible for his actions and behaviour. I wanted my sweet and happy powerful self back, and I left him.

How did I change? First of all by realising that what had happened and what had caused this was I had been trying to fix him. I did not yet know that people need to want to be healed, fixed or better.

We are all born with our positive power strong and pure and powerful.

Little by little things happen to hide this power and we must dig deep to find it. We must shed layers. He had become my project. However, by really evaluating my life, I realised the positive power of choice. What choices was I making, who was I spending my time with, what was I doing? Where was I directing my energies? No-one had been forcing me to spend time or chunks of my life with these people from my past. Then deciding in little steps to make positive changes in my life, I went to see a famous personal development self-help success speaker named Jim Rohn and learned about setting goals and working harder on yourself than you do on your job. I began reading a lot more; books such as *Think and Grow Rich* by Napoleon Hill and *The Game of Life and How to Play it* by Florence Scovel Shinn. I weeded the garden of friends and slowly began hanging out less with drama creators and more with positive and creative people with kindness and compassion. I began regularly reading positive books, working toward my dreams, doing volunteer work so instead of trying to fix others I was truly making a difference in the world. And pretty rapidly my life began to change for the better, and then I began to have more and more positive power and it began to just naturally flow in and out of me. I met the guy of my dreams and am now happily married with two girls, a house by the beach and an amazing career where I get to uplift, encourage and help others, until I was just living in my full positive power! I also realised how much of my life I had tried so hard to be perfect. I began to research and study how to develop more confidence. I also started to apply all that I had learned.

In 2010 I quit my entertainment career and launched my coaching business and created a confidence course, a life coach certification program, wrote bestselling books, hosted several shows, co-hosted a podcast and so much more. I also had my daughter Nia in 2012. Life was so great, rewarding, and happy. I was helping people, growing as a person and all was going well. I also learned that you never have to be perfect. There is no such thing.

'Even when life has tribulations or problems, focus on the gifts that come out of them during and after. Next time a big problem or hardship appears; do not label it that, look for the gifts right away, still feel the sting of it, yes … but begin looking for positive solutions and taking action, and that problem or hardship will become a blessing, gift, growth opportunity and actually amaze you in many ways. Rise above hardships by getting up and physically moving, emotionally talking to a loved one, going for a walk in nature or even taking a bath, and mentally staying focused on what is good. Heal from guilt about your past. Forgive yourself and take action to be better, do better and use past mistakes to be wiser. It does no good to keep punishing yourself. Instead, use it as fuel to be great! Sometimes you need to learn who you don't want to be, so that you can be your best self.'

Then suddenly In 2017, I started to feel extreme symptoms that I had never experienced before, pretty much two weeks out of every single month on average I had nausea, heart racing, insomnia, extreme physical flight or fight panic, feeling anxiety that often lasted nonstop for days, joint pain, headaches, etc … My hormones would go haywire. It was to the point that I would feel too sick to do things. I missed so many trips, events, nights out with friends. Luckily I would often have two to five weeks that I would feel good or at least pretty good in-between all of this regular madness. Also, my parents, husband, kids and family were extremely supportive. This all caused a lot of distress, PTSD and fear of symptoms, because they were so harsh. I never knew from one day to the next if I would feel horrible or not. I was also experiencing a type of grief from missing out on so many things. The panic and fight or flight anxiety with heart racing was the worst.

All the while I began to search for solutions, trying a multitude of things. Over the course of six years, I saw over twenty-five doctors, specialists and healers, many of them great, but just still not finding the solution. I had misdiagnoses, wrong medications and the confusion of never figuring out what was wrong. I did acupuncture, herbal programs, diet changes, hormone replacement therapies, the pill, thyroid, heart and hormone doctors, healers, massages, IV therapies, you name it. Many of these things had symptoms themselves. I gave each a long, full try, with each thing fizzling out without success. Nothing was working. Was I going to be like this forever, when would it end? What was going on? It felt crazy and baffling. During this, not one doctor or specialist suggested that it might be my breast implants.

In 2020, the pandemic was in full force. My kids were learning at home. I was working from home. I was enjoying the extra time with my family. We love being together. It had already been three years of experiencing these same symptoms with no solutions.

Although I had never been a big drinker, I was desperate for relief and I had gotten in the habit of drinking wine at night or on days that my symptoms were extra bad, and it would actually help to make the symptoms lessen, helping me get through the days. Desperate, I started to find ways, sometimes crazy ways, to drink more amounts more often, especially with flare-ups, even with my family telling me to stop. It got so bad sometimes that I would just drink to pass out, too overwhelmed with how badly I felt that I literally couldn't handle it. My body would feel like glass cutting throughout me. This resulted in the unimaginable; several trips to the hospital, only being told I had too much to drink and then several trips to detox/rehab places. This was very hard on me and my family. I would never consciously choose to behave like this. The doctors, counsellors, nurses, etc. all would tell me over and over that I didn't have an issue with alcohol and that I was just self-medicating. I would stay in a facility, which was uncomfortable, scary and extremely humbling and unreal, but because I didn't understand it was a true issue and still had no solutions, I ended up repeating the issues. I committed to stopping, and even completed the AA twelve-step program, which was very healing, and to this day have never had another drink and do not want to. I also ended up finding an amazing psychiatrist who specialises in hormonal disruption and imbalances and found medications that have helped to some degree, but not all the way. Plus, I was taking more medications than I ever would have imagined, the goal being to taper off of them and not need them anymore.

In 2023, I was seeing an amazing therapist, healer and intuitive who told me that she was intuitively seeing something heavy and toxic that needed removing in my chest area. I still didn't put two and two together until a friend talked to me. My friend who went through similar symptoms pointed out that she thought it was breast implant illness and gave me the long list of symptoms that can come with it. Although I had seen mention of it before, I didn't realise there was a list of over forty possible symptoms. Basically, your body rejects foreign objects in your body – yes, even saline implants – and I realised that I have had about sixteen of those symptoms, including disruption of hormones, and in early 2023 decided to get them removed. I got referred to an amazing surgeon in Newport Beach who had a calm and positive bedside manner.

I felt reassured and safe that this was the right decision.

In April 2023, I went through an intense six-hour surgery. They removed the implants which I was told had been recalled to potentially cause cancer. They scraped out scar tissue that had formed into what is called capsular contracture on one side, so part of that had to even be scraped off my rib (this causes mould or bacteria to travel into your body) and I ended up getting a fat transfer and lift. After going from a size D to an A again, your body needs a little assistance. In the first few months after surgery, recovery has been challenging because I have had a lot of detox symptoms that can make you feel sick. This can happen when you first get them out because your body is detoxing the bacteria or mould from the scar tissue. However, I am so glad that I got those foreign objects out of my body. I do not need that to feel confident, pretty, sexy or enough.

I am on the right path toward feeling like my vibrant, go-getter self again. I know with time, I will feel all the way back to my energetic healthy self. More women need to know about the dangers of breast implants and the havoc they can cause. I would have never gotten them had I known. I know it is all part of my life's journey and I have definitely learned to be a strong, brave warrior, am so non-judgemental to others, have an even bigger amount of knowledge and wisdom to share and help others with.

Although this has all been extremely challenging, I always trust in my journey. I trust that there is a huge purpose, gifts and learning involved. Throughout this path, I have gained a lot of wisdom, strength, bravery, resilience and tenacity. I no longer judge anyone, whether someone is struggling, hitting rock bottom or feeling low, I have a much deeper empathy and understanding. Recently I helped talk a man who was on drugs out of wanting to commit suicide, I have talked about this journey on podcasts, in posts and in helping others in person. I know this was not an accident. I have a deeper understanding and compassion for myself, overall life and others. I have hit bottom many times, and climbed back up, increasing my faith in God and my power. I have also learned to let go and let God take over. I am inspired to see where my journey goes next and hope to help as many people possible.

KIM SOMERS EGELSEE

Intuitive, Life & Business Coach, Ted X Speaker and Author

Connect: kimlifecoach.com / @kimlifecoach

KRISTI MAGGIO
GOD'S PLAN IS PERFECT: THE FAITH, PERSEVERANCE & RESILIENCE OF A WOMAN ON A MISSION

A s I sit here today and put pen to pad, I fear I must confess that I begin writing with a feeling of defeat, even though I am far from defeated. These are the moments I am sure we all have had, are having or will have again, especially when you are on a mission to change the world. However, no matter how big or small your mission may be, it can be frustrating when you give yourself every day and do your best going above and beyond, putting in 1,000% of your whole self just to be set back by various things that you encounter along the way. I wish I could say that once you get 'on a roll' moving forward everything just falls into place naturally and continues to do so, but the reality is that the greater the good, the bigger the mission, the more difficult and challenging life seems to become. What keeps me going and what keeps me waking up every morning at 3am is that I know in my heart I am fulfilling my purpose. The purpose and plan that God has called me to fulfil. Do I wish it was easier? Yes. Do I wish I could walk away at times and never look back? Yes. Then I ask myself, *If you do give up for the easier way, would you be happy?* No.

You see, life is all about the choices we make. Each decision, whether good or bad, propels us forward or sets us back. We consistently encounter a world that masks its flaws, presenting a facade in order to hide its reality behind closed doors. Our focus often lies in how others perceive us, rather than authentically portraying our own truth. We meticulously curate snippets of our lives for social media, but how much of it is genuine? Do we seek validation from others rather than embracing our true selves? I, like many others, am guilty at times of this charade. If you were to peruse my social media, you may see me as a success story, maybe not. Indeed, I have achieved success, but not in the conventional sense of fame and fortune as society would define it.

To truly understand the essence of my story, you must grasp the significance of authenticity. Life is not about imitation, conformity, blending in or adhering to societal norms. As a faith-based person who believes in God and attempts to live like Jesus, which is not an easy task, it is stated best in Romans 12:2, 'Do not conform to the pattern of this world but be transformed by the renewing of your mind. Then you will be able to test and approve what God's will is – his good, pleasing and perfect will.' It is about following the compass of our true selves, standing out in our uniqueness and taking the road less travelled – the one set out by someone greater than us all. So, is your will and your purpose led by your heart that is so strong that you have no doubt in your mind that this is the path you were meant to follow? Or is your purpose and will led by what you want the world to perceive you as, who society tells you, you should be? These are two very important questions to find your true north, so to speak, the true calling for your life. Because if you are living a life and working towards a goal that is being dictated by how the world will look at you, you will most likely not be able to overcome the challenges you will face getting there. Your why must outweigh everything else, because the road to success in whatever you want is not paved for a smooth ride.

My journey as an entrepreneur began ten years ago in 2013 at the age of thirty-five. At this time, I had no idea that I would become an entrepreneur, nor did I really know what one was at that time. As a teacher for many years, I moved to the Dominican Republic to perfect my Spanish. Initially, I had planned to stay for only a year, imagining myself returning to the United States to make a meaningful impact in inner-city schools that I felt I could do the most good. Armed with my freshly acquired administrative degree, my aspirations were to become a principal or superintendent. I wanted to change the system that I had been fighting against for so many years, and I thought this was the best way to do it. I truly believed this experience would give me an edge to secure employment in urban schools, most with large Hispanic populations. So, I took a sabbatical from my current teaching position, and I set out to spend a year in the Dominican Republic.

The biggest question I get most often from people is, 'Why the Dominican Republic? Why not some other Spanish-speaking country?' It was an easy explanation that few could understand unless it had ever happened to them. Exactly a decade earlier, while in the country on vacation, I had felt an undeniable energy – a pull, almost – that I was supposed to be there. It is really inexplicable, the draw that you feel, a feeling of excitement, as if the world around you is shifting. It happened again when visiting in 2006 and again in spring 2013 which was the last time I visited before moving there. At the end of that vacation, when leaving to go to the airport, I passed by a school, and that is when it hit me like an overwhelming blow to the head to find a job in the Dominican Republic. Everything between April 2013 and July 2013 lined up so serendipitously that I knew it was meant to be.

Within a few weeks of my arrival at the beginning of August 2013, I met someone and fell in love. Yet, it was more than love that anchored me to the country; there was something much greater, and that was the realisation of an untapped market for quality education. This was the beginning of what ignited my entrepreneurial spirit. The traditional education system had never aligned with my beliefs. I saw it as a flawed structure designed to mass-produce knowledge, stifling individuality and unique talents. My hope of making a difference within the system faded, replaced by an unwavering conviction to create my own educational paradigm. I had to start an alternative system; a revelation that did not occur overnight.

The conclusion of my first school year in the Dominican Republic brought about a tumultuous turn of events. In this challenging situation, as a single woman without family, in a foreign land, it would have been understandable for anyone to consider running back home. The school owner, known for intimidating and coercing her employees, attempted to frighten me into remaining at the school. However, I refused to be bullied or tolerate unfair treatment. Consequently, I received advice to pursue legal action against her, not out of a desire for financial gain, but to convey a powerful message that her mistreatment of vulnerable individuals was unacceptable. I refused to be silenced, and by taking this stand, I hoped to empower others to raise their voices as well. Fear and intimidation do not sit well with me, and I have always been one to fight for what I believe in and be a voice for those who feel they don't have a voice. It took six years, and three appeals on her part, for me to get that point across and win the case, which just goes to show that while the system may work slowly, faith, perseverance and a lot of patience does pay off in the end.

Now, upon leaving the school, I began private tutoring from my apartment, which allowed me to learn more about the people and what they were looking for in the area. Word of mouth worked its magic, and my roster of private tutoring clients grew steadily. I eventually was working seven days a week almost twelve hours per day. In the process of discovering what direction to turn, I came to understand a great many things. So, my initial vision to open an English language learning centre became a distant idea as I uncovered a discouraging reality. Adults who professed their desire to learn English, often lacked commitment, making their attendance sporadic at best. In stark contrast, young learners consistently attended, propelled by their parents' unwavering support, and it was during this time that my dream of opening a language learning centre expanded into the realm of starting a school. This is where we must realise that what we originally envision can change, but that does not mean that you throw in the towel and give up. It just meant that you take what you know and pivot in a different direction.

After this realisation, my journey was filled with intense emotions, reflecting the struggles, commitment and occasional loneliness I experienced due to being misunderstood by my family. Most often it is those closest to you that try to put doubt in your mind, usually because they don't understand why you are doing what you are doing and because they love you and think they are protecting you. They thought I was crazy and persistently urged me to return to the United States. I somehow allowed myself to feel irresponsible, as if I was a child unwilling to grow up. Their idea was that I could have a comfortable life earning much more money as an administrator and a good retirement plan. When people discourage you from pursuing your dreams and ambitions, you must stand firm by constantly reminding yourself why you are doing it in the first place.

Determined to make a start despite lacking funds, I continued day in and day out with my private lessons. While I had made a few friends in the area, my relationship with my boyfriend was also fraught with turmoil. Although I won't delve into the intricate details here, I felt incredibly alone and frequently betrayed. The only thing that kept me going was my unwavering faith in God and in my inner voice assuring me that I was on the right path. The burning desire within me to effect significant change was a relentless force; I continued driving my mission forward, as well as the desire to be my own boss. Financially I struggled, barely making enough to cover my rent and basic survival needs. Many nights, my dinner consisted of eggs and rice, the cheapest of two staples that had nutritional value, and once every two weeks, I would take the bus to the supermarket, as I didn't own a car, and to ease the challenge of carrying multiple grocery bags on the bus, I devised a practical solution – I would bring a small carry-on duffel suitcase. This way, I could conveniently place all the smaller grocery bags inside it, ensuring I had enough supplies until my next shopping trip. Pretty savvy, if I do say so myself!

After nearly three years in the country, I felt utterly lost and hopeless. I was on the verge of surrendering and giving up entirely when a glimmer of opportunity unexpectedly presented itself. A woman in the area expressed her intention to transition out of the school she had founded, and the building would soon be available for sale or rent. Knowing I could not buy it, I engaged in negotiations to rent it, and over the course of two months it seemed as though everything I had been working towards was finally coming to fruition. However, just as everything seemed to be falling into place, she abruptly withdrew, stating that she wasn't yet ready to close the school. I got the news as I was standing outside on the corner waiting for the bus, and I broke down and cried in the middle of the street. I was mentally, physically and emotionally exhausted. It was as if all the effort I had poured into preparing for this moment had been in vain.

On that same fateful day, I called my lawyer, ready to abandon the idea of establishing the business, and I started preparing my mind to begin looking at job postings back home for the coming school year. I told my lawyer there was no point in proceeding with the paperwork because it seemed it wouldn't work out. However, he convinced me to persist, emphasising the importance of having everything ready when the opportunity arose. Reluctantly, I agreed, thinking more about the money it would cost that I didn't have to waste on business documents I wouldn't need, and my faith was dwindling. That afternoon I went to sign the papers, feeling dejected and questioning why I was wasting $600 on something I didn't need.

Upon returning home, I prepared for a class, and when the child arrived, the mother brought her daughter inside, and I shared with her the unfortunate turn of events. Desperately, I inquired if she knew who owned another location, a small building that appeared to have been a school but was now closed. I wondered who the owner might be. She reluctantly said no, and I put it all out of my mind for the next hour taking refuge in the company of my young student.

Upon the return of her mom, she came in with some astonishing news. She told me that in the past hour she did some investigating and found the owner of the school I had mentioned. He happened to be at a restaurant nearby and wanted to speak with me. Hope flickered once again, and without hesitation, I went to meet the gentleman. This encounter took place on a Friday evening. Saturday morning, I visited the location, and by Monday, I had signed the lease to rent the school. Here, I realised the truth of a biblical verse: 'When God opens a door, no-one can shut it; and when He shuts it, no-one can open it.' The revelation struck deeply, for I had been tirelessly pursuing the other school, but God had closed that door for a reason – a reason that would soon become clear.

Filled with a mixture of excitement and disbelief that this was all finally happening, I borrowed money from my mom to gather all the essentials necessary for starting the school. It should have been a time of pure joy and celebration, and to some extent, it was. I poured my heart and soul into preparing the school, ensuring everything was immaculate for the grand opening. The outpouring of support from friends and well-wishers was heartwarming, as they offered their assistance in any way they could, but then came the bittersweet moment that I never saw coming. It was like being punched in the stomach and attempting to catch your breath which you can't seem to find as you gasp for air.

Amidst the joy of opening the school, my heart was simultaneously torn apart from within. The person who had brought both immense happiness and profound sorrow into my life for the past three years, the one I loved beyond a shadow of a doubt in that moment because he had helped me prepare everything to get the school ready, up and left without any warning. He had just received his visitor visa for the United States a month before, and a week before the school's opening, the school that we had painstakingly readied together, investing equal amounts of effort, had vanished. He never bothered to inform me. There was no goodbye, no explanation.

The mixture of emotions within me was complex and contradictory. The triumph of the school's inauguration clashed with the anguish of a sudden and unexpected loss. Bitterness mingled with the sweet memories we had shared, leaving me in a state of profound sadness and yearning, falling into a deep depression. I cried myself to sleep for weeks only to realise weeks later that for him and his family the 'American dream' was a greater opportunity than a life with me. It is the dream of most Dominicans to be able to go to the United States one day, and I was just a means to an end. If you have ever had your heart broken and you didn't see it coming, then you will relate to the utter feeling of loss, as if someone you never imagined being without suddenly died tragically and you never got to say goodbye. I now realise that sometimes people come into our life for a season, and when that season is over, we must let them go. I know he was meant to teach me a great many things about the ways that this country worked and what I needed to know if I wanted to thrive and not just survive.

As the school year began with only seven students, I had also found three English-speaking individuals to join as teachers, envisioning an English immersion school. However, they lacked formal training as educators, so I had to do a lot of training and much of the work. The first year we had students from pre-k, kindergarten and first grade. At this time, I was using a borrowed motor scooter from a friend to get back and forth from my apartment to the school, and I was still tutoring from my home full-time. Once the school opened, each morning I would open the school, welcome the teachers, leave the snacks, then return home to tutor throughout the morning. I would then diligently prepare lunches bringing them back to the school, before resuming my tutoring in the afternoon. Once I was able to purchase a car thanks to the help of my uncle, I started providing transportation services to make a little extra money, and therefore in the first year, I was a teacher, administrator, curriculum coordinator, secretary, chauffer and cook.

This is the aspect of the entrepreneurial journey that often goes unrecognised – the countless hours of work, struggles and difficulties, as well as the loneliness of doing everything yourself and having few people to talk to because most think you are crazy for doing what you are doing. If your mission isn't deeply rooted and your understanding of its purpose and potential outcome isn't resolute, the path will be too difficult and you will most likely quit. This serves as a vital lesson for aspiring entrepreneurs, particularly the younger generation, who embark on the path of starting their own ventures. It is essential to recognise and acknowledge the often-overlooked aspect of the entrepreneurial journey – the immense dedication, perseverance and countless hours of toil that lie ahead. Without a profound sense of purpose, recognition of the challenges you will face and a steadfast understanding of the potential outcomes, the road ahead will be too difficult.

An intriguing turn of events unfolded at the end of the first year; the lady I had initially negotiated with to open the school the year before, made her decision final to close it. Seizing the opportunity, I secured and rented the original property at a lower cost than before. This serves as a powerful reminder that sometimes when our plans don't align and our ideas face setbacks, it's because they weren't meant to be at that specific moment. By persistently pushing forward and remaining adaptable, we open ourselves to alternative paths that may lead to even greater success. It's important to understand that while everyone desires the grand vision and lofty dreams, we must first lay a solid foundation and build incrementally. Each brick laid contributes to the strength and resilience of the structure. This realisation guided my journey, starting with a humble group of seven students.

As I transitioned to the new school, the following year, I continued to grow. By 2020, the school had expanded up to the fourth grade, with eighty-five students, and we began to outgrow the space, as it resembled more of a preschool or a facility for younger children. Parents expressed their concerns about the limited room for older kids to play and explore, signalling the need for a larger and more suitable environment.

As usual, divine intervention came into my life, and I had the opportunity to meet a gentleman who owned a digital radio channel called Punta Cana Hits in the local area. Interestingly enough, just a week prior, I had been contemplating the idea of hosting a radio show, and almost miraculously, within that short span of time, he approached me, seeking an English-speaking radio host. When he asked if I knew anyone who would be interested, I couldn't help but suggest myself. To my delight, he agreed without hesitation. This one show opened a multitude of doors for me. I began hosting the weekly show, *What's Up Punta Cana with Kristi Maggio*. It provided me with the opportunity to connect with new individuals, conduct interviews and feature diverse guests. Little did I know that this would eventually lead me to a remarkable chance – an interview with a highly esteemed figure within the Dominican Republic.

To my surprise, it turned out that my brother-in-law had a connection with a gentleman he worked with, who happened to be best friends with the highly esteemed figure in the Dominican Republic. This revelation came to light during my visit to Virginia for Christmas in 2018, where I was invited to a Christmas party hosted by this gentleman. We engaged in conversations about my life in the Dominican Republic and his deep friendship with the prominent figure. Little did I know that he would become a crucial ally and friend in my journey. This man became instrumental in helping me understand the intricacies of business and my aspirations to establish and build a new facility for the school in the Dominican Republic. Up until that point, I was still renting the property for my school. Once again, God was at work as this man wholeheartedly believed in my mission and recognised the impact I aimed to make.

Amidst all this planning for developing the new school location, I was tirelessly managing the daily operations of the existing school, overseeing a team of teachers, developing curriculum, designing social media content, producing a radio show, organising summer camps and more. Every aspect of the business was under my supervision as I worked relentlessly to bring it to life. Yet another glimpse at the behind-the-scenes efforts that often go unnoticed.

However, all came to a halt in March of 2020. I took a significant risk during this period by making a deposit on land to build the new school without having secured the investment to back it, and I found myself scrambling to prevent the loss of the deposit I had placed on the land. Unfortunately, I was unable to gather sufficient funds for the first payment, leading to the forfeiture of the deposit.

Even amidst the challenging circumstances, I remained dedicated to providing the best education to the students. I worked tirelessly, coordinating virtual classes on platforms like Zoom, conducting live English and Spanish lessons twice a day on YouTube and preparing learning materials. Despite my efforts, many parents chose to abandon the school, leaving me in overwhelming debt. This financial burden made it impossible for me to pay the rent and settle my outstanding bills. Consequently, I made the difficult decision to close the school by the end of June 2020, uncertain about the future and feeling a mix of frustration and disappointment.

In the face of these challenges, I had to release all the teachers from their positions, providing them with the necessary severance payments. While I was unable to fulfil all financial obligations, I remained steadfast in my commitment to never use COVID-19 as an excuse. My determination was to eventually repay every penny owed to those who had supported me along this difficult journey, and I did, but my spirits had once again plummeted, questioning why and not understanding how something I had put so much time and energy into could just come crashing to the ground. Something I knew was placed on my heart could seem as though it would never truly happen. This is where the journey of learning and self-development begins.

I was introduced to two books by a woman who reached out to me at random on LinkedIn, *The Science of Getting Rich* and *Think and Grow Rich*. These books may appear focused on money, but in reality, they taught me the principles of creating success. It wasn't about the money itself; rather, they instilled in me the ideas and strategies to achieve what I wanted, and thanks to those two influential books, I found a way to regain my footing and reestablish my focus. I started recording daily inspirational messages that were aired on the radio, and I resolved to study the lives of successful individuals, much like Napoleon Hill had done. By doing this, I gained invaluable insights which motivated me to resume my radio show, and it also sparked the idea of writing a book.

I visualised all these aspirations and plans on my vision board, and I prayed a lot. The emergence of Zoom as a communication platform allowed me to conduct interviews with people whom I would have never been able to meet in person. Zoom became the new medium, enabling me to connect with individuals from various backgrounds. I sought to improve myself, deepen my understanding of business and become a better individual overall.

While I was inspired and being fulfilled in my personal growth, everything else was still in the depths of despair, and I found myself back at my mother's house at the age of forty-three. I had to apply for social assistance, and I hid from the world trying to portray I was still someone that I was not. People would say, 'Just get another teaching job, it's okay to move on, you tried, and it didn't work out, it's not your fault.' But it was my fault, and deep down in my heart, I couldn't give up, because the mission was too great.

Despite not having a stable job, I managed a few tutoring sessions here and there, barely scraping by as I sought to learn, grow and explore every possible avenue to get back on track. It was during this time that I realised something profound in the education space. What initially seemed like a plan to have a single school in Punta Cana, Dominican Republic, now had the potential to become a global model. COVID-19 had rapidly accelerated technology, connecting people even in the most remote areas and presenting an opportunity for me to provide education on a much larger scale. I began engaging in mentoring sessions with youth from different parts of the world, and this brought me a great sense of accomplishment, taking my mind off my own situation and focusing on helping others, especially young people. Surprisingly, I discovered that I was learning just as much from them as they were learning from me. Remarkably, I found myself inspired, and I managed to start a podcast, host an educational summit and write my first book, titled *Follows and Likes: Is This All That I'm Worth?* by the end of 2021.

However, once again amidst my aspirations, something tragic occurred that shook me to my core. My father fell ill with COVID-19, and merely three short weeks later, on 21 November 2021, he passed away. It was a devastating blow, and I couldn't help but feel immense anger towards the system that would not allow anyone in to see him, to the ridiculousness of not making certain proven remedies easy to obtain, to myself not doing more and being consumed by fear and self-absorption. I still blame myself to this day, but the only thing that gives me solace when I do is my faith and understanding that God's plan is incomprehensible and that He has a reason for everything that happens. While I would much prefer my father here with me today, I know he is with me in everything I do.

It was through this heart-wrenching experience that I began to see the blessing concealed within the failure of my school and the crumbling of everything I had built. If my school hadn't failed, I wouldn't have had those precious last few months with my father. We wouldn't have shared our morning coffees together, engaged in our usual arguments about my career choices. He simply wanted me to return to teaching or take up an administrative job, but I knew deep down that I couldn't. Unfortunately, my father fell ill on the day my book was published, and he never had the chance to see it. Yet, with time, I have come to appreciate the silver lining in this painful chapter. The time spent with him was a gift, and it has provided me with a fresh opportunity to restart the school and rebuild financially because of what he left behind.

After spending five months settling the necessary affairs following my father's passing, I mustered the courage to embark on a new journey, and in April 2022, I returned to the Dominican Republic with the intention of reopening the school, and reopen I did that September. At the time of writing this, the first year of the school's reopening has come upon me, and I am filled with a profound sense of gratitude and joy. While the struggle is still undeniably real, the reward is equally significant.

As this chapter draws to a close, an incredible ending unfolds. Alongside my journey, I accomplished yet another remarkable feat – I published a book featuring twelve extraordinary young change-makers, inspiring others with their stories of transformation. This book soared to become an Amazon new release bestseller, highlighting the incredible potential within these young individuals and the multitude of others like them who are reshaping their lives. My mission remains steadfast: to ignite belief in the hearts of youth, empowering them to realise that they can achieve anything. I now stand on the precipice of completing accreditation for the revolutionary education program I am creating. This program will grant students from any corner of the world a United States diploma, coupled with a specialised area of expertise, and creating young students that are 'future proof'. When I embarked on this entrepreneurial journey, I never fathomed the title of 'entrepreneur' would find its way to me. Yet, I have come to understand that an entrepreneur is, above all, a problem-solver – a lesson instilled in me by one of my mentors.

How can I impact the lives of one billion people? How can I create a business that uplifts, transforms and empowers? For me, the answer lies in the realm of youth – the ones born into circumstances where traditional education fails, where they feel confined and unable to flourish. My purpose is to unlock their true potential, allowing them to transcend the limitations imposed by society's narrow expectations. So, I implore you, dear reader, to embrace your own journey, whether you find yourself amidst its winding roads or are just taking your first steps. Uncertainty may prevail, and the destination may elude your imagination. A decade ago, if you had foretold the extraordinary events unfolding today, I would have dismissed them as implausible. Yet, through faith, perseverance, unwavering determination and a mission fuelled by obsession, the right path reveals itself.

I leave you with this last question that I am often asked, 'Why do you work so hard?' In this, my response remains unwavering – I do not do hard work, I do HEART work, because nothing is ever hard when it comes from the heart.

KRISTI MAGGIO

CEO, Maggio Multicultural Academy
Connect: kristimaggio.com / @kristi.maggio

SOMALIA BROWN
LOVE HURT ME TO LIFE: MY JOURNEY FROM SELF-SACRIFICE TO LOVE MASTERY

O ne split second. That's all you have. One split second to choose her life or yours. At the blink of an eye, you jump in the pool to save your friend's sister's life after she fell in even though you don't know how to swim. She is nowhere to be found and the water is slowly covering your entire body. You have no idea what is transpiring and can't see because your eyes are squeezed so tight, it instantly gives you a head-ache. You're frantically gasping for air trying to swim back to the top to no avail. Now you're stuck, drowning and sinking further and further down like a heavy rock to the bottom of the pool. That was me at the age of six.

I'm drowning and I can hear voices faintly in the background scream-ing. They pulled my limp body out of the water and laid me on the concrete. As they delivered the news to my mother she was in total dis-belief. Her body became paralysed and she couldn't move. Somehow, she mustered up the strength to pray and yelled out, 'Not my baby girl! NO NO NOOOOO!! Not my baby. Please don't take her from me.' My mother continued to cry out, while my father rushed to my side. He's experienced being under extreme pressure before as he served in the Vietnam War, but this was different. THIS HIT HIM DIFFERENT!

He remained calm while assessing the situation and began CPR until the ambulance came, but on the inside, he was doing everything he could to hold it all together and not fall apart. He looked down at my lifeless body in his arms, lips turning blue, and his heart ached at the thought of losing me. In despair out of sheer love for his baby girl, he pounded on my chest yelling and calling my name, 'Somalia, come back. Come back to me, Somalia.' Numerous thoughts ran through his mind. *What if I never see my baby girl's smile again? What if I never see her run again or dress up or kick a soccer ball?* He wasn't ready to let me go!

My earthly father was saying come back to me and my heavenly father was saying you have to go back. In that moment two parallel universes collide, mirroring one another – as it is in heaven, so it is on earth. Both my fathers were on one accord and to this day, my heavenly father will use my earthly father to speak to me all the time and I know when it's my daddy and when it's God. Because of my choice, I sparked a chain reaction in my parents, but especially my earthly dad. In one moment, I triggered a new-found love from both which deposited the strength and rawness in vulnerability to become this container of love you see before you today. This was the beginning of numerous rebirth cycles in my life which led to learning the lessons and mastering love.

Can I challenge you to shift with me and see how you have had countless mini rebirths throughout your life which have all collided at the same point in time to bring you to this book? A book full of inspirational stories we have sat on that will encourage you to be true to yourself and others. For a lot of people when they hear the word rebirth, they assume it's just a once or twice in a lifetime experience. For example, when someone gets saved or has a spiritual awakening, they see it as a rebirth, a one-and-done. Yes, we are new creatures but that doesn't mean it stops at getting saved or enlightened. As if we won't have to go through anymore experiences that will birth another transformation – another rebirth. A rebirth can occur at several stages in our lives. I know mine did. However, I have come to know through experience they are life lessons with many moving parts, facets of the story and personal development which leads to mastery. For me, it was in the area of love. I was constantly being stripped of what I thought love was in society's eyes and being reborn with what God said love is. This is the story I've been sitting on that many need to hear. I hope my journey of rebirth in love encourages people to look at their own lives and see that they are nowhere near the same as they were two years ago.

Looking back, I realised that rebirth isn't exactly what I envisioned. It is starting again from a point of renewal, a point of being made new. With each rebirth He killed a version of this world's love that was not serving me, that shouldn't have been there and replaced it with a new love. I have encountered rebirth at multiple stages in my life, and boy they have not been pretty at all. Some were amazing, and I was all for it. I ran to it! Others I dodged, ducked and hid until I realised I needed them. At six years old, I drowned and my encounter with God changed me. I went through a rebirth. A factory reset, if you will, and I went back to the original me that I was created to be. The version of me that was birthed into this world to change and defend mankind. Not the curated version of me in the world that was shaped from various experiences.

On my journey to mastering love, there were three main lessons I learned: stare love in the face, fall apart to become something new, and allow yourself to be stripped and stretched. The first lesson happened when I died. Even when I made the decision to stare love in the face and help the drowning girl, that was me standing in my truth of rebirthing into a selfless person with love for others at any cost – including my life! That was a heavy decision at such a young age but was so easy at the same time. My second rebirth was at the age of eighteen when I found out I was pregnant. My first thought was, *I don't want this.* I was young and selfish. My parents were ready to be grandparents, but I wasn't ready to be a parent. I was good with my decision until I was invited to church and a little girl went on stage to read a poem. The poem was about all the babies in heaven whose parents didn't want them. Boy, the sucker punch I received was the gut-wrenching I was feeling. I jumped up mid-service and ran to the bathroom. I looked in the mirror and said, *Are you talking to me? Wow, that hurts!* Mind you, I don't know who God is at this time, but this overwhelming peace came over me. Did I understand it, no, but I sure did embrace it as He dismantled my heart and this version of love to become the presence of love.

Fast-forward and my last track meet to make it to district is upon me. I had to sit out two weeks to heal before I was allowed to run again. One day my mom said to me, 'Slow down! Do you not understand what you just did? What your body just went through?' I looked at her and kept moving. Right before I stepped on the track to run, I said, 'God, if you truly forgive me for what I've done, I will make it to state even if I get third place.' I ran my race and at the finish line I threw myself on the ground with tears in my eyes. That race hurt so bad because of all the raw emotions I was experiencing throughout it. *Am I gonna make it to state? Does He forgive me? Do I want to know if He really forgives me? Etc ...* I think I cried the whole way, which by the way makes it super hard to breathe while running, but I made it. On the ground head down, I looked around and I finished in third place with no practise for two weeks which was a miracle and impossible. I was racing against the best in the district to make it to state! God had shown me that He forgave me and that I can forgive myself. I realised the work it took for me to bounce back in two weeks created a standard. This sparked the rebirth of the healing love in my life. I had to learn through sacrifice, that this fiery love was written in my DNA. This was through self-love, but not the typical way we understand self-love.

The last part He needed to work on was my heart. I had to be reborn to be who I was truly created to be. I had to lose myself countless times to find myself and love. I had to be more vulnerable to let others in and to fully allow these rebirth cycles to occur. In order for me to embrace being the container of love, I had to empty out everything I had known about love thus far. Everything I learnt through my parents, relationships, friendships etc. and that was at times devastating to me.

I learned that through these experiences in my life I was called to demonstrate a level of love many are scared to experience because of the prerequisite. Love had broken me only to repair me. It taught me about honouring others' silent needs and requests, not just the loud ones, genuinely. The power I found in love was giving of myself deeper than surface-level loving. I had to give the very essence of who I was and be willing to expose myself countless times not knowing if the recipient would receive it or not! Matter of fact, the hardest lesson was loving those I didn't think deserved it and still doing it. But the greatest reward was being able to give that love to someone I did honour and respect. The one who satisfies you, the one who takes a little bit of courage and the leap to match your love. The one who shows you your mess and challenges you to change. The one who is tied to your mission. The one it was all worth it for, the one who has the same mission to teach others about this new real love. This is the current journey I am on, one of self-mastery and love of another. It is a journey to be the ultimate container of love in its purest form. In order to impact those closest to me and assigned to me, I had to give all of me. Why, because love looks like death on a cross! Per a conversation I had with one of my accountability partners, their take on true love is it's not always pretty; it's messy, heavy and yet filled with beautiful scars and battle wounds that remind you of just how much each one means.

The tears I have shed and the fear that almost overtook me and tried to hijack my body repeatedly, is what forced me into becoming a container and a presence of love. In this era, my charge on this earth is to bring this level of love to earth. I also discovered my endless capacity for love without boundaries or reservation. My capacity to hold this authentic level of love increased in me ever since I acknowledged it was there all along since birth.

I didn't know I was going to learn a new version of love and those lessons I learned were the toughest of my life. I had to master those lessons, not just learn and go through them. During those lessons I learned I'm a spiritual pioneer and forerunner, which means I have to blaze a trail and face things first without a blueprint. I have to fall, make mistakes and come back to share a love that's never been taught.

The past two weeks of my life I was placed on a spiritual timeout to see just how much I've grown in the last year. I was in a trial by fire that I had to go through alone and overcome. There was no other option, and guess what the area was – LOVE! I had to unlearn an old version of love and relearn how God loves – not how the world loves. Just like you, I was created with a great purpose. Your purpose may not be my purpose, but we were both placed in this earthly realm to fulfil that purpose. For me, it was living in the love dimension so I could shift the atmosphere of the people I was around. This is the basis and the epitome of a 'defender of humanity'. I trigger those around me because I am designed to lead and heal. This is what I was created to do. Maybe you were too? And if not, whatever you were created to do, go fulfil your purpose in this realm.

The time set apart revealed principles and nuggets I was able to apply to my life immediately as well as revelation:

My DNA is being rearranged and moving in the earth.

Heal first, even though everything looks like it's falling apart.

I must heal so I can hold space for those assigned to me. Once I'm healed, then I can lead and teach my collective group.

I'm not traditional and nothing about my calling is.

I am to uplift and harness love to shift atmospheres, situations and circumstances and bring in unconditional love the right way.

I must heal and love in a way that I'm willing to say, 'Love sees no blemishes in one another.'

I'm being prepared to last and I'm meant to be in alignment.

Love is not passive but demands a response.

It's not just giving of myself on the surface but giving the very essence of who I am.

I must be willing to expose myself countless times not knowing if the recipient will receive it or not.

Be open because they may not receive it and respond how you expect.

He placed a mirror in my face as often as needed, to help me walk in unconditional love, courage, peace, trust, resilience, patience, forgiveness and transparency. Unconditional everything in all areas of my world. I had to learn to release it all. When I say everything, I am not only commissioned to walk in love but BE unconditional love. That means I am willing to look past all blemishes known or unknown and integrate love and healing for me, those connected to me and others as well.

I allowed love to disrupt my life, by having unconditional transparency again and again. This new fiery love reached down to the depths of my soul as though I was a child. It merged with my life force of boundless energy and connectivity to the heavenlies, and now speaks through my vulnerability. It gives my life force a different voice which heals those I encounter.

I now understand why love is so controversial, so misunderstood in our world. This was God's big plan all along to get me to shed all of society's norms, ideals and everything I was so attached to – what I thought love looked and felt like. I had to be stripped, stretched beyond recognition and shed countless layers that masked the real version of the love I had to give. After this process, I was no longer connected to this world. I could now be used to fulfil my purpose of defending this realm and the least likely of us all.

I was also challenged to soften my love and fine tune it. By doing this, I became the container for more love. I was repeatedly placed in situations to remove my old ways of how I viewed love, therefore, increasing my capacity to love authentically. Every old idea I had about love being of obedience and power contributed to me not feeling worthy of love. He showed me how others demand love and how others, including myself, didn't really know or understand love. He exposed me to a love I now have and increased my capacity to receive, plus the courage to give it away so I can always be a conduit to receive more. It is the law of reciprocity at its finest. Fiery love was born through mastering the art of letting go of my idiosyncrasies of self-love, letting go of the world's concept of love and how to give love. Vehement love was born through shifting my mind from the shackles of what the world perceived as love, to finding freedom through surrendering and my sovereignty in Him.

Every rebirth was a disruption that catapulted me one step closer to who I really am. Love was not what I thought it was; it was more than I bargained for, and I would do it all over again changing nothing. Love showed me what I was not, then pushed me to be that very thing while experiential learning taught me how to be the container and bring divine love and abundance to all those who meet me, including myself. In this season of my life, I couldn't research love. I had to become it. This is mastery.

I had mini mindset shifts in my rebirths of choosing to love over fear, I began to see a pattern that if I didn't choose to love I would repeat the cycle. I finally understood that if I stay in love, I will always elevate in God, stay in peace and joy. All the countless rebirths have granted me access to unlimited love marked with a redeeming grace in my life. My heart beats with a frequency of God on this earth to disrupt and dismantle hatred, bitterness and anger. The power love has is infinite. I now know I cannot lose sight of the end goal, I must go through every rebirth cycle to understand the value of love, how it opened me up to receive an empowered love and to choose love over everything, no matter the cost! Love is an investment that hurt me to life, what has it cost you?

SOMALIA BROWN
Defender of Humanity
Connect: LoveHurtMeToLife.com / @realonesomalia

IMPERFECTLY PERFECT
CAMPAIGN

The overarching aim of Imperfectly Perfect is to change the face of mental health by dismantling the stigmas associated with it. These stigmas tear at the very fabric of society where the very elemental courtesies for human decency are forgotten and eroded.

One stigma utilises a language that proposes that mental health starts and ends quickly. 'Snap out of it' is a phrase often heard as a satisfactory treatment in the torrential battle of mental health disorders that engulf lives. The scars of mental health disorders are very real and behind a face that from the outside you think is doing okay, there is a conversation we do not want to hear or listen to.

Stop for a moment, if this were someone you loved, your brother, sister, wife, husband or friend, how would you champion them in their constant battle?

By changing the culture and challenging the perceptions of mental health awareness, Imperfectly Perfect captures the essence of humanity by helping the world to see there is a serious issue that has no barrier of fame, fortune, social status, creed, beliefs, ethnicity or age. Their innovation is centred with founder Glenn Marsden who captures the visceral emotion frame by frame, tear drop by tear drop. Glenn's heart knows, truly knows, the plight through personal experience. With that heart he is breaking ground and forging new paths.

We urge everybody to join Imperfectly Perfect and some of the world's most influential public figures to build a legacy – your legacy that surpasses time. A legacy that provides education, healing, support, advocacy and public awareness so that the conversation around mental health disorders normalises, enabling your children, grandchildren and future generations to live without stigmas attached to mental health.

To find out more about Imperfectly Perfect campaign, simply head to the official website at:

imperfectlyperfectcampaign.org

All enquiries to: generalenquiries@imperfectlyperfectcampaign.org

The ImperfectlyPerfect podcast can be found across all major podcast platforms.

You can find our global efforts across all social platforms at @ imperfectlyperfectcampaign

Milton Keynes UK
Ingram Content Group UK Ltd.
UKHW010916230124
436534UK00005B/340